Embrace Your Space

Inspiring Stories of Reclaiming Home

Benjamin S. Albert, JD, MBA & Elizabeth B. Hill, MSW

with Gabriela Campos, Lianne Dixon, Mara Dowler,
Donna V. Finocchiaro, Christina Fitch, Sheri Giancarlo,
Aina L. Hoskins, Janet Johnson, Rosemary King,
Audra Garling Mika, Rachel Schemmerling, JaneSTORM, and
Mary Ann Waterman

Green Heart Living Press

Embrace Your Space: Inspiring Stories of Reclaiming Home

ISBN (paperback): 978-1-954493-16-2

Cover photo and design: Teresa Hnat

Dedication

To our children.

Table of Contents

Dear Reader,

The piles can feel overwhelming.

Love. Joy. Family. Friends. Hopes.

Dreams dreamed. Plans planned.

Projects started. Projects stopped.

It can all feel so much.

This stuff of life.

Wherever you are, we are with you.

It doesn't have to feel so hard.

You don't have to do it all alone.

You deserve the space to breathe and be.

Love & Reclaiming,
Elizabeth

Introduction

Benjamin S. Albert, JD, MBA

Unique to many books with a foreword or introduction, this book is all about moving *forward*. Here, people share their stories about how they moved a direction other than backwards, even if it included movement to the left or right, or even in a circle. Forward. And in telling these stories, the authors hope that by sharing their most intimate secrets and experiences they can help you to "embrace your space."

Though each experience with "stuff" is different for each author, and undoubtedly for you, there are common threads: We all have too many things. Material items that have been collected during a lifetime of any length impact our mental health. We ascribe value—sentimentality—to items in a way that ignores both their original purpose and the reality that things have an expiration date even when not explicitly stated. If we do not, someone will have to deal with our stuff. And ultimately, there can be freedom from the weight of stuff, ours or others.

Herein are journeys that should inspire. These are the words of people, not unlike you, who have faced challenges and prevailed. As a group, we hope that you will read, find your motivation, start your walk to a better existence, and learn not to let things control you, your life, and your limited time each day.

I came to the world of organization by accident. My first client was part of a dog playdate in my backyard who, after asking to use my bathroom, called bullshit on the idea that my house included children and a pet because of the organized state that it existed on a random Saturday afternoon. Organization has become a passion because I recognize—often in the notes that I receive or in the teary hugs that are genuinely offered by clients—

how much nearly all of one's life improves when they can embrace their physical (and by extension, their mental) space. After years of coaching folks, I now understand both the typically silent weight stuff has on people and the relief that surfaces after some smart work and a commitment to change. What the authors here share is so important on many levels, but for everyone it should allow for meaningful conversations and a spark to make changes.

In the pages that follow, you will read about heartache, courage, loss, love, resolve, grit, and determination. A quick skim might suggest that these stories are about just stuff, but the reality is that these authors have exposed the rawness at their core; the rawness that often helped them to make changes in their lives. It is the hope that the stories of these authors encourage you to face the piles in your home, to have tough discussions with loved ones, and mostly to recognize that, if you choose, you have more power than the things anchoring you to an imperfect life. Read these stories. Celebrate the successes. And then, make a plan of your own to embrace your space. We're rooting for you!

With Encouragement and Belief in You,
Benjamin S. Albert, JD, MBA, DAD

www.EmbraceYourSpaceCT.com

Chapter 1

Embracing Your Space

Benjamin S. Albert, JD, MBA

I had a roommate—the kind that you get when you say "I do" and legally move from "I" to "we"—who might be described, politely, as disorganized. In her defense, my great love for her when we dated was blinding enough that I elected to ignore the major disorganization "red flag" that she waved in front of me. (Picture her standing on a heap of stuff while unfurling the warning flag!) I ignored a lot, and asked her to marry me.

In the formative days of our relationship, my naiveté about mental health issues, my genuine interest in building a life with her, and, in particular moments, my desire to be intimate with her, allowed me to enjoy temporary blindness to certain realities. In one carnal moment, I rang her Brookline apartment buzzer at 81 Green Street. Caught off guard by my request to come up to her apartment, she stuttered and stammered about wanting to see me but her "apartment was a little messy." After promising that I did not care (truth) and not knowing how much I would care about her clutter one day, she invited me up. It was only upon exiting her bedroom to head home that the funky apartment smell enveloped me while my eyes grew to collect the piles of paper, books, art supplies, clothing, bags, and, impossibly, piles of piles.

With the backdrop of even that single example, it would be reasonable to conclude that I knew what I was getting into when I dropped to a knee and asked her to spend our remaining years together. But, clutter and the impact that it has on one's soul is a metastasizing problem. It grows. It spreads. And more like a fire than cancer, it steals the oxygen that a soul survives upon. It can kill a relationship if not managed. It did, in part, for us.

I cannot accurately define the moment that *her* clutter started to hurt me. It was more like the oft-cited boiling frog fable in which the frog complacently lets himself be boiled. That biologically inaccurate story is used to warn about a slow threat, and that warning would have been appreciated by me. I did not notice anything for a while. Love, as they say, is blind, and I was blind to what her choices meant for me and us.

Certainly, I remember the weekly notes to Theresa, our cleaning lady, with some version of:

> *Hi, Theresa! Hope you're doing great! There's a new bottle of [insert name of some new, unproven, claimed to be "green" product with no evidence to support it actually cleaned] on the counter. Please skip the guest room, the office, and 'Child A's' room this week. Thanks!*

Even though we were paying Theresa, and her progeny in subsequent years, to clean the entire house, clutter prevented such activity. Rooms were literally designated as off limits for a given week... or weeks.

I also can remember the arguments and empty apologies when clutter would interfere. One week, bags were deposited by the front door. I reminded my "partner" on one Monday that we were having company—another couple—over on Friday night and asked that her welcome-to-our-messy-home bags be put away. (One bag contained expensive work equipment from a hospital so I was loath to touch any of it.) On Wednesday, I gave a gentle reminder that we were heading closer to host mode. When Friday arrived along with our company, and the husband tripped over a bag at our front door, I bit my tongue, made a joke about it, and set a fuse for the anger bomb that would explode once we hugged our friends goodbye that night.

I can remember (because a physical scar remains to this day) slicing the tibial skin of my leg when trying to maneuver through her boxes that congested our finished third floor. One might argue that the cardboard containers were filled with useful items. That argument would, however, be wrong. The boxes were planted like seeds in a desert when we acquired the home. They went untouched until she vacated the premises a decade later. They brought no value; they took but did not give.

More than anything, I can remember the fights. I can remember the tears. I can remember my pleas that I wanted a "happy home" even though I could not articulate then how the clutter, the disorganization, and the related promises and lies made me physically ill and emotionally exhausted.

She will contend that the divorce was in no way her responsibility. But, that position just confirms both lack of growth in the aftermath and a failure to look at the reflection in a mirror. Her stuff and her choice to prioritize stuff over people had a deleterious effect on our relationship. For me, the divorce and the physical garbage that she literally abandoned in our family home gave me a chance to learn. Though I lived in the marital home, post-divorce, without making real changes for over a year. I even left her discarded sneakers in our shared closet and her unread copy of "Fifty Shades of Gray" in her nightstand. I eventually recognized that I needed to make the space mine, and to convert the *house* into a safe and calm *home* for my two children.

With a stated goal of purging her emotional fingerprints from the house, I started donating, recycling, and throwing away her stuff that continued to absorb positive energy in my home. Previously, I had attempted to give her bags of luggage, clothing, books, shoes, etc., but those transfers of garbage bags filled with her shit also resulted in attitude from her and unnecessary engagement. Remarkably, rooms started to seem bigger and nicer. The kids started to grow into spaces that were previously defined as off-limits explicitly or implicitly by their mother and her choices. The house was cleaner because it could be cleaned. The air was less toxic and we started to revel in the freshness of the space. Our cleaning ladies—two absolutely delightful and caring women—offered regular comments, support, and comparison of how we "once lived." My heart was regrowing in sync with me learning to make the simple choices that resulted in that seemingly elusive happy home.

Even though my goal of ridding our space of her was finite, the results were numerous. The kids started to compare our flower-filled, music-enhanced, and laughter-frosted living space with what they had to endure in her new home. The children reveled in keeping their space clean and in reviewing what they wanted to keep, what fit, and what might be beneficial to donate. My heart filled.

There were other unintended consequences. I can remember the day that my then eight-year-old son asked me to hang a picture. Within a minute, I had the tools and wall hook. He made a head exploding gesture and asked, "How do you know where everything is?!?" We talked (and there have been several conversations with my kids since then) about organization, getting a job done, reducing stress by owning one's space, etc. I know that I have a job to do in preparing them for life on their own, for their future relationships, and for ensuring that they work for a happy home. And, I know that teaching them means unteaching some bad habits that they learn elsewhere.

Another surprise from my efforts brought us here, to this page. To these words. A new-ish friend had joined me in our backyard for a puppy playdate with her dog and ours. At one point, she needed the bathroom. I gave her directions and stayed outside to chaperone the dogs. When she returned, she exclaimed, "Don't you have kids?" She knew the answer so I was confused. She could not get over how neat and organized our home was on a random Saturday afternoon when the dog date was a somewhat impromptu decision. She excitedly cross-examined me about our home and then insisted on a full tour. Throughout our brief investigation inside, she shared both amazement with how we lived and how peaceful it seemed, but also how disappointed she was in her home. She confessed to her house being an embarrassment, and that it was not what she wanted for her family. To my surprise, she asked if she could hire me to help her family. Though I had shared with no one before, I had done lots of research on decluttering and organizing. It was, however, just for me.

That friend became my first client. Over the years, helping people to live real lives—demanding lives filled with children or grandchildren, pets, jobs, and a whole host of responsibilities— while living in happier spaces has been joyful in a way that I could have never imagined. I am not sure that I'll ever be able to thank my ex-wife for subjecting me to the craziness of clutter and disorganization, but I will thank myself for putting in the time and effort to learn that there is a better way; that it matters if one embraces their space.

Today and anchored to humility and compassion that can only come from living through my personal experience, I hold people's hands, give many hugs, and coach them to embrace their homes, offices, and workspaces. I receive the most touching notes (and unnecessary gifts) from clients who speak about family engagement on a new level, friends being welcomed in their homes for the first time (or *proudly* for the first time), and how relationships with partners, parents, and children have flourished when decluttering revealed bright sunshine and healthier oxygen. Like any successful athlete, the real work is done by the client, but I get to share the glory of living a happier life as the coach. I am grateful for so many who have welcomed me into their home, who have shed honest tears in front of me, and who were willing to learn and invest to make their spaces, and lives, so much richer.

To be clear, I am not famed organizer Marie Kondo, and I don't want to be. My goal for my house and those of my clients is a real-life grade of B+. I want company to feel welcome with no warning. I want my kids to be on-time to their commitments (clutter prevents such). I want to be able to find what is needed with no stress. And, I do not ever want to waste a few hours or a weekend cleaning my home. The way we live, and the way that I teach my clients, means freedom. And happiness. And healthiness. As I always say, physical or mental, it's your space. Embrace it!

About Benjamin S. Albert, JD, MBA, DAD

"A jack of all trades is a master of none, but oftentimes better than a master of one." While some misunderstand and dismiss the true intent of this quote, the full phrase is directly applicable to Benjamin and the underlying reason for his success as a coach. People speak of "wearing different hats," Benjamin has actually done so. He practiced law at the highest level, and spent more than a decade guiding litigants, corporate leaders, and anyone who needed assistance even if they could not afford his talents. For nearly four years, he coached patients in their physical and mental well-being while wearing a white coat and stethoscope. He has saved and grown client businesses, and has guided employers to create better and more successful work environments as a consultant.

Ultimately, his vast and deep experience supports why the "jack of all trades" reference was intended to be a compliment. Benjamin is a generalist rather than a specialist. He's versatile and adept at many things. And, as his clients know, he is remarkable at coaching people to be their best. Helping people declutter mental and physical spaces has become a critical part of his professional journey.

Benjamin lives in Connecticut with his favorite two short roommates, Ysabel and Dylan, and their adorable rescue pup DOG.

www.EmbraceYourSpaceCT.com

Chapter 2

Reclaiming the Matriarchal Palace

Elizabeth B. Hill, MSW

"We are artists. We don't clean."
"A clean house is a sign of a sick mind."
"Only boring people have clean homes."
"We pile because we have so many interests."
"House cleaners have sticky fingers. Can't be trusted."

I've heard the words above more times than I can count. This is my family lineage—from my matriarchal side. It is deep in my bones. Even though my piles have caused me stress and panic attacks, they also served as visible proof of my artistic temperament, revered in my family. I was let off the hook from regular cleaning of anything. We have an epic and beautiful family history, but it is so beautiful that it feels painful to look at because of all the love lost and secrets kept.

I've gone through many reconfigurations of my life, all of which have called for decluttering, clearing, and releasing. Leaving belief systems, roommates, a twelve-year marriage, relationships, jobs and careers, have all provided rich opportunities for clearing.

This chapter of my life is about family, love, trust, and breaking the chain. It is about taking a stand for my family's health and well-being. It is about getting help to do what I (and the family) were not able to do on our own. It is about taking a stand for love in a way that might not always feel very loving in the process. It might not be pretty. It might mean getting dirty. It might include tears. It might feel like a kick in the gut. But, it is most important to do.

This story is about me embracing the space of my grandmother's home which was built in the 1800s. The structure is 2,800 square feet, not including a one bedroom apartment with a loft space. Two years ago, I moved into this home with my two teenage children. I have bought two homes in my life, both tiny capes. I call our home with Grandma the "matriarchal palace," because after living in two "cozy" homes, this place feels like an absolute mansion. As of this writing, my grandmother is 97; she was 95 at the time of our moving in.

Before I moved into Grandma's house, my mother was the primary caregiver of my grandmother for over three years. My mom slept there every night, and cared for Grandma every day with the exception of a few hours for a few mornings each week when a caregiver visited so mom could go to her home and have a break. One day, my mother called me at work saying she was having chest pains. She thought she was dying. I could tell she was having a panic attack. This was my wake-up call that the then-current situation of caring for Grandma was not okay. We had pushed the limits of this arrangement to the breaking point. It was a crisis upon a crisis.

During the same time, I had also pushed the limits of my home situation to the breaking point, both financially and emotionally. So, I decided to start tiptoeing into Grandma's to help more. And to see, if in doing so, I could make space to let my family care for me a bit.

Easing In

When I first started sleeping at Grandma's, I slept where my mom slept—the brown leather couch in what we called the "scintilla room" after the tiles that lined the floor. The leather couch was laid out with sheets, two blankets, and two pillows. This was the place my mom carved out for herself to sleep.

There are four bedrooms upstairs, all of which were unused. Before I moved in, the beds, closets, and bookshelves all held evidence of mice. Lots of evidence of mice. The couch was the only "safe" place to be.

At the table where my mom, aunt, and Grandma frequently ate, there was a pile of silver in the center surrounded by piles of stuffed animals, cards, playing cards, crayons, notebooks, and pens. It was an altar to my Grandma. It could not be touched.

Before we moved in, I started bringing the kids over on the weekends so that we could see if this living situation was doable. This also gave mom a two-day break and gave us time to do more cleaning up of the home before we moved in. It was a gradual clearing process. My children were 12 and 13 at the time. I kept them away as best I could from cleaning the gross stuff, but they helped immeasurably with the heavy lifting of furniture. Sometimes I would ask them just to sit in the room with me, so I had company while I sorted through the piles. (I would tell them their only job was "emotional support." They could play their games, watch their show, read their book, they just needed to be near me while I figured out what the heck to do.) They also helped by being a stand for what we as human beings deserved, which was a clean and comfortable space to live. I don't like to admit that they were this stand for me, especially as a social worker and coach. Some chains I could break before I had them. Some chains are theirs to break. I aim to make peace with this.

The cleaning and clearing process was hard. We didn't want Grandma to think we were doing anything. She hadn't allowed anyone to clean in decades. I decided that it didn't matter, we had to take over. We needed to step in. In order to even crack the surface, we had to get some things out of the house. At first, we snuck things out of the house so Grandma did not know. We'd go out a side door or shut doors so she couldn't see. The painful truth (which I didn't realize when we started) was that hardly anything was salvageable. Most things just needed to be thrown away. Grandma would have thought we were stealing, but we were really throwing out things that had been eaten or peed on by the rodentia.

Divine Intervention

One day, the ceiling collapsed. We hired people to rebuild it and—HALLELUJAH—this brought us a dumpster. I felt the ceiling collapse was divine intervention because it got us a dumpster for a legitimate reason. When Grandma asked, "Why is that horrible thing in our driveway?" I could reply, "The ceiling fell down. The people that are fixing it need it to put all the stuff there."

We had been sneaking stuff out, doing dump run after dump run. It felt such a relief to have a dumpster. The kids, my mom, and I filled the dumpster with soiled pillows, broken furniture, moldy records, and 40-year old toys that had been half-eaten by mice. Throwing stuff in the dumpster was so much easier than doing these small, one at a time, runs. What I wasn't able to do myself (order a dumpster and face the horror of my Grandma) was done for us.

After that, my daughter Raven, the youthful voice of truth and reason, said to the whole fam-damily, "We need another dumpster." She just said it. Flat. I felt my lower back freeze up and my stomach turn. At that time, I couldn't even imagine speaking those words out loud in front of my grandmother (I have granddaughter privilege in this household, but Raven has great-granddaughter privilege which is even MORE powerful!) Since then, I've gotten better at speaking up for the things I need and want. I still get the back freeze-up and stomach turns sometimes, but it's worth it.

Getting Help

Benjamin Albert appeared in my life at exactly the right time to help me through something that I just could not face on my own. He persuaded me to let him help me. I was a hard no at first.

And then, I realized, somewhat painfully, that God was trying to help me through him. So, I said yes.

I convinced my family to let me hire him to help us make the house a healthier, cleaner, more organized home. I told Grandma he was helping us make the home more beautiful. (If I had said organized she would have probably kicked me.) Grandma is a big fan of aesthetics.

We tackled one room at a time - starting as far away from Grandma as we could and then moving closer. We'd face a project, then I'd need to escape into an easier project for a bit, before returning to the hard stuff. Benjamin stood (and sometimes kneeled) by my side as we faced one conundrum after another. There were definitely times that I shut down and just sat staring into space.

I cried pretty much every day we worked. Oddly, often after we had completed a project and a room looked amazing, I would start crying. I would cry for the way things were, how long we had lived in another, completely unnecessary state of filth, clutter, and decay. I cried from feeling the weight lifting off, and being so unfamiliar with the feeling, I didn't know how to cope with it.

In my own work with coaching clients, I often want to let them off the hook. They are often so hard on themselves, already. I don't push. I am the coach to hire if you need a gentle hand. My clients will push themselves - and I will be there when they decide to take the leap.

For my home project, we didn't have time to wait for me to be ready. Benjamin pushed me; albeit with humor, hugs, and lots of "quick like a bunny" encouragements. I hated when he pushed me. And I am so grateful he did. If he wasn't here, I would have left the drawers of things untouched, I would have just floated through the surfaces. The closets would still be filled with unusable and filthy clothes—because for some reason I just couldn't bear to face them alone. He pushed me, using loving support the whole way.

I know over time that on my own it could have at least looked aesthetically better, but I would never have faced the layers underneath. I would have still felt the weight of the filth in the closets and drawers, so I wouldn't have really felt free.

When Benjamin came in to help, I had already done a great deal. And it was not enough. I had hit a wall. It was clear I needed someone else to help me make the hard choices.

What I'd accomplished by then was make the bedrooms basically liveable, but there was still so much clutter that we basically had no room to move around. My son's room, for instance, had seven chairs in it. Seven chairs. Yes, James had a clean bed to sleep in and a small space for his clothes. But who can feel comfortable in a room with seven chairs?

Piles abounded: piles of toys, TJMaxx gobbly-gook, cards, books, everywhere. There was a wheelchair that no one used in the living room piled high with magazines and bags. There were gift bags of Christmas presents in the living room. There were chairs that were so feeble that no one was allowed to sit on them, but no one was permitted to throw them away. There were so many piles that cleaning was impossible. Bookshelves were filthy and had evidence of rodent visitors. Seven of the eight closets in the house were unusable because they were filled with stuff that was eaten by rodents. There were drawers and drawers of things that no one touched.

As I cleared, I would give myself a moment to hold the items and treasure them, before sending them to Goodwill. I would feel love for my family and know that by letting go, both of resentments and physical objects, I was demonstrating love to my family and myself. When I felt I couldn't give something away because "I might need it someday," Benjamin would gently remind me that someone could use it and really appreciate it right now and it would be a loving choice to let them. This shift in mindset helped me immeasurably.

As we moved through the rooms, we revealed the beautiful

sculptures made by my grandma's mother. Many of these sculptures are of family. As we cleared the knick-knacks, we could actually see the beautiful art made by my family. We could appreciate the gorgeous antique tables and chairs now that we could see them. We found photos of my great-grandparents and my grandparents (all knock-outs!) that had been stuffed in drawers. I found a painting of my great-grandfather, James Work. Benjamin helped me place this portrait above the fireplace. I cleared a table of unused electronics, notebooks, and magazines, and placed pictures of my parents, my grandma, my aunt, my children and my nieces and nephew. With the liberation of family art and photos, it felt like all of our family was finally settling in and living here in peace. Our souls could all take a breath.

Now I look back to life before Benjamin's help and I can't believe we were living like this. Memory is a funny thing. I feel like our home has always looked the way it does now. When I look at the "before" photos, my entire body tenses up. I feel awful that my grandma and my mother lived in this environment for about three years before I moved in. I wish I had stepped in sooner and taken a stand for my mom. For my grandma, too, but especially for my mom.

When my daughter talks about how horrible it was before we moved in, I cry for my kids and for myself. I'm in the process of forgiving myself for it. Writing this is part of that process. I didn't know I could stand up to my grandma and be successful. I didn't know that if I just stood my ground, that the family (after their initial freak-out inspired by fear, mistrust, and hatred of change) would completely accept what I was doing and thank me for it. I just didn't know what I didn't know.

As I write this, I wonder: Have I truly embraced my space? I still want to escape a bit. Living in a family home and caring for a 97-year old who is as stubborn as Katherine Hepburn is no joke! But I have embraced our space in this place we call home. I know that I am choosing it for this time, for the love of family, and myself. I embrace my children and know I am providing a clean, creative, loving, and peaceful home. I know now what it really means to embrace my space and I know that I can bring that to whatever places we call home.

Now that the house is liveable and I can breathe the air, I feel much calmer. My kids and I spend time together. I'll hang out with the kids and we'll watch a movie together. It changed the way we relate to each other. Before we made these changes, we'd all be in our separate rooms. We didn't have a space for us to eat together that felt clean. Now we regularly have family meals together. In fact, we have TWO clean tables we can eat at now - one in the dining room and one in the kitchen! We actually "hang out" together! My kids are fourteen and fifteen now and it feels a grand achievement.

Benjamin says his house is a B+ and I affirm. It doesn't look like a Better Homes and Gardens photoshoot, although it could without much effort. It looks beautiful, cared for, and loved. And, it feels comfortable to be in. You aren't afraid to sit on a couch for fear of messing it up. It is a place of peace, creativity, curiosity, and laughter.

If Benjamin's house is a B+, mine is probably at a B- most days. I'm an overachiever, but in this case, I'm overjoyed and proud of my B-. Our home had a big ol' F before, not even close to passing. I was terribly ashamed of it and would only let my friends in that were in the "known me for 20 years and aren't going anywhere" category.

I now know where things are, so I don't lose time finding them. When I get a new appliance or electronic, I immediately put the manual in the binder that is in its designated place for it. I have room in closets and places to put things. My creative projects grow piles (i.e. when you work on 10+ books at a time, piles are inevitable), but they are now kept in check and are easily organized.

I've gotten better at talking with my mom, my aunt, and my grandmother about what we need for the home. My mom and aunt have been tremendously helpful. My grandma—who we thought would kick and scream and hate everything (she did)— now says every single time she walks through the living room "it looks very good in here, doesn't it?" I told Benjamin that symmetry was extremely important to Grandma, so he made sure we wove that through each room. She comments on the little figurine ducks laid out on a table, because she can now see them, undistracted by clutter.

As I write this, my new house cleaner is cleaning our home. I've never had anyone else clean my house! I couldn't have even imagined having someone in to clean my house before because of the clutter.

My dear soul friend through all the lifetimes Karla Archambeault has moved into the apartment in the home. She helps me care for Grandma and helps take care of me. She said recently, "I remember the moment when I knew I could move in here." When she said this I started crying. If Benjamin hadn't helped me conquer this work, Karla wouldn't have ever chosen to be here. I am so proud of myself for doing what needed to be done for her to feel she could be here with us. She did so much work to clear and clean the apartment before moving in.

This has been a story of learning to accept help over and over again. The universe kept sending the message until I learned. Before, I had to wait for divine intervention to get help for my home. My first lesson was to learn how to recognize the help as that. Now, I am on the lookout to ask for help. And I've done so. By seeking out an ideal housecleaner, by asking Karla to move in, and by asking for help from my mom, aunt, and children, I have used my voice to make our lives better. I have learned to embrace the spaces within and without. And we're all breathing easier for it.

About Elizabeth B. Hill, MSW, ACC

Elizabeth is the CEO and founder of Green Heart Living and Green Heart Living Press. She is the best-selling author of *Success in Any Season, The Great Pause: Blessings and Wisdom from COVID-19, Love Notes: Daily Wisdom for the Soul,* and *Green Your Heart, Green Your World: Avoid Burnout, Save the World and Love Your Life.*

Elizabeth coaches clients on mindful leadership and writing to heal, inspire, and grow their impact in the world. Trained as a social worker, yoga teacher, and ontological coach, she weaves creativity, spirituality, and mindfulness into her work with clients. With over 15 years of experience writing and leading collaborations in the nonprofit sphere, Elizabeth brings a uniquely engaging approach to collaborative book projects. Elizabeth lives in a matriarchal palace in Connecticut with her family and the neighborhood bears.

www.greenheartliving.com
www.greenheartlivingpress.com

Seeking Safety

Aina L. Hoskins

"Feng Shui is like acupuncture for your architecture. It aligns your energy and creates flow."

Mary Ann Waterman

"My room full of possessions; They remind me of who I used to be back then."

Gabriela Campos

"External shifts start happening around you because you choose to create a beautiful internal vortex of love and positivity."

Chapter 3

A Necessary Sanctuary

Aina Lee Hoskins

I was eight years old, my room was large and full of natural light. My bed was beautifully made along the wall. My coloring desk was in the corner overlooking the room. I had a sitting area with books and dolls. My closet was filled with my clothes hanging color-coordinated while the shoes were lined up in a row. Everything was clean, neat, and organized. My room was beautiful both physically and energetically. At this young age, I intuitively placed my furniture and my belongings in locations that made me feel good and safe.

I lived in a large home with my mom, stepdad, and two older sisters. It was a chaotic household filled with sexual abuse, mental illness, alcohol, and a lot of fear.

Even though I was very young and still a child, I knew that to survive I had to create a sanctuary for myself that consisted of order, beauty, peace, and safety. I believe I was born with an innate knowledge of a higher power and universal energy. I utilized Feng Shui to create calm in chaos as a survival mechanism.

I had an organized closet where I created a little sitting space and an altar, where I put small items that were important to me. I also would reorganize my room so that I was in what I'd later learn was called a "power-position" in Feng Shui. This created a feeling of calm within the chaos and safety in a hostile environment. It was something I had control over. I was also the "good girl" among my sisters. I was studious, I followed the rules, had order and just wanted everyone to be happy—including me.

When I was a teenager, I started realizing that things weren't "normal" in my household. My older sisters had moved out and I was the only one left to deal with an abusive stepdad and a mentally ill mom. At age 16, I decided it was time for me to move out and focus on me and my studies. My mom agreed to pay me an allowance until I finished school, so I moved into a small studio apartment and continued my studies.

Again, I created a beautiful space with great energy where I could study and live my new life as a young adult. During this time, I learned to budget and track all monies so that I could focus on school. I knew that I needed to release and let go of what was, so that I could create space for something new. This resulted in me becoming estranged from my family for a while. It gave me space to develop into who I was meant to be. I finished my schooling with an MBA in Finance and Business Psychology.

I created a successful career in the corporate world. However, I found myself in an abusive marriage. As history was repeating itself, I had a clean and beautiful home but there was chaos around us. I created a warm and welcoming home for my children and their friends. This abusive marriage resulted in me almost losing my own life. If it wasn't for my then 11-year-old son, I wouldn't be here today to share my story. The blessing here is it forced me to end the marriage and have sole custody of my three children.

It was time for another fresh start for me and the children. I just had a knowing that I needed to clean and clear out the negativity in my home so that we could thrive. Was it obsessive? Was it OCD? Or was it the universe having my back and teaching me how to create a sanctuary and a safe place in the midst of chaos and turmoil? That which once helped me to not only survive but thrive, could also become a way of life and a potential career.

As I was working on my own healing, I started studying and became certified in psychology, universal laws, transformational life and business coaching, spiritual finances, and Feng Shui. It was amazing to see that so many of these modalities had been a part of my practice since childhood, not to mention they had saved my life and sanity many times.

I loved the idea that your environment is a reflection of your energy and if you alter your environment, your life can change. I had seen some of that play out in my life, but this was big! Feng Shui had been my survival mechanism. Now I was studying Feng Shui, giving talks on how to elevate your bottom line with Feng Shui, and helping clients create a space that welcomed prosperity and abundance.

The number one rule in Feng Shui is declutter—that was not foreign to me. I loved to clean and declutter. I felt energized, it helped clear my mind and kept me grounded during times when things easily could have taken me down another path. We have all heard that a cluttered environment creates a cluttered mind. It doesn't allow for new energy or new creative thoughts.

I started playing with this intentionally. I drew up my home using a Feng Shui bagua (an energetic map of your home that shows different areas of your life in your home). I made sure that my wealth corner represented what I wanted to create – financial flow. I deliberately made sure I slept in a power position (having the best visual of the room) to help give me restful and peaceful sleep.

Then came the realization that everything is energy and if everything is energy, well, that means so is money. I had always organized my money in my wallet, it faces the same way, and it goes from smallest bill to largest bill. I also kept a record of all bills and tracked my spending. Again, another innate knowledge that had served me well.

What became clear to me is that the way I treated money could change my relationship with money. I made sure I loved money, I kept it neat and tidy, I always had a beautiful wallet that housed my money in a respectful and responsible way. When I paid my bills, I wrote thank you on the checks and paid them with gratitude. I gave thanks to the providers of services that I paid. When paying for groceries I gave thanks to everyone who had played a role in providing them to me; from the farmers to the pickers, to the truck drivers, to the grocery store workers. I thanked them all! I found that living in gratitude would give me more to be grateful for.

Today Feng Shui is a part of who I am. It allows me to create a beautiful, safe sanctuary for me to live in. Feng Shui helps provide a space for me to be creative and productive in my office. It helps to create the energy of love and peace in my bedroom. I am fully aware of the energy in my space. When I don't like the energy, I have the power to move some things around to change that energy into something I desire.

What helped me survive in childhood became a tool to create a life I love. What I used to help me feel safe and in control as a child has evolved into practices that allow me to shift my energy easily and effortlessly. When we go through any kind of loss or trauma, we develop tools to help us through. This was a tool that saved me. It was a tool that I utilized. It was a tool that may have had control over me at times, however, now I have control over it and utilize it to help me on my continued journey.

About Aina L. Hoskins, MBA

Aina L. Hoskins was born in Oslo, Norway. She achieved her MBA in Finance and has over 30 years of experience in the corporate world working with mergers, acquisitions, and budgeting. Aina is also an administrator for a charitable trust.

Aina has studied with many world-renowned teachers and is certified as a Transformational Life Mastery Consultant and Coach, EFT, Reiki, Feng Shui, Kinesiology, and many different prosperity programs.

As well as being Executive Officer at Squadron Capital, Executive Managing Director for eWomenNetwork CT, Aina is a speaker, success coach, and finance and Feng Shui consultant. She is passionate about helping women regain their power, shine their light, create prosperity, and accelerate their results, so we can all create lasting success.

Chapter 4

Diary of a Personal Archivist

Mary Ann Waterman

My room full of possessions
They remind me of
Who I used to be back then

My father told me that I had a space problem. That seemed like an astronomical conundrum. There was just not enough space for everything. My childhood room was not a place in which to live, in the sense of everyday life. It was, instead, a place to keep all of the things that I felt defined me while I continued on with the important work of constructing myself. I felt as though to lose a thing, a material object, was to lose a part of myself.

I kept dutiful notes in calendars of important events, written in small, black ink. I played with the power of memory, and the ability to inhabit the past. I saved flowers which represented rituals, connected to certain, perfect moments in time. My relationship to things was highly emotional; it was fixated on the nostalgic.

I was a collector. To collect is first of all to gather. With each new object that I acquired I felt better, safer, more content. The shiny pencils, the fun erasers, the vending machine bouncing balls. My daughter looks at my collections for what they are, a group of nice things; she asks if she can write with the pencils. I had never considered this, to use the objects practically. For me my collections had been something more. A way for me to organize my universe into something over which I could exert a little control. To possess something beautiful, of value, so that I could become the same, both beautiful and valuable.

Maria Montessori explains that children "incarnate" their environment, "The things she sees are not just remembered; they form part of his soul."[1] My grandmother's house in Vermont, where I had spent many summers, is still quite alive to me: the blue painting of the old covered bridge down the street, the woven rugs in the kitchen, the pink and green dishes in the built-in cabinets in the dining room. Interwoven with these memories of things is a connection to mythical small town life in the village of Lyndonville. There was an old schoolhouse down the street where my mother and aunts once walked to school. Later when my aunt and uncle wanted to transform the family property into a Bed and Breakfast, I staged a full-scale rebellion.

I have at times felt that it was physically impossible for me to leave a space. One summer was spent almost entirely in south Florida in the house with terrazzo floors and yellow patio furniture on a large screened-in porch. I had my own room with two twin beds. We had been in Boynton Beach about twelve weeks when it was time to drive back to Connecticut to start school. At eight years old, the summer felt like eternity. I continued to ride my bicycle around the driveway in those final minutes before our imminent departure, deeply uncomfortable with the weighty sense of limbo. Ultimately, I decided that I could not part with my heavy down pillow that I had slept on for the last three months. I kept it on my bed at home for the next twelve years.

In 2015, with about three weeks notice, I decided to move to Spain. I had been speaking with a friend about what he might enjoy in Europe. He suggested that I live abroad for a year. I looked at a teacher website I had used in the past and found a posting for a job in Valencia, Spain hiring for that spring. Soon, they had offered me a position and it was off to the Consulate in

---

[1] Montessori, Maria. *The Absorbent Mind.* Radford VA, Wilder Publications, 2007, p.56.

NYC with just a little bit of time to pack a couple suitcases, leaving the rest behind.

* * *

When I took a last look around at my storage room full of things before we sold the house, I asked myself: *what did I still need?* There was a moment that afternoon when I had opened a drawer full of t-shirts which I had saved from the eighth grade. Thirteen was probably my most ritualistic and shakiest year in terms of a grasp on reality. In the same place and arrangement within the drawer as they had been, the power of the object was magnetic. Strong I had needed it to be then; these favourite shirts had anchored me. Now, though, they threatened to take me back to a place that I did not want to go.

After experiencing the freedom of a new country, and a culture less attached to stuff than America, I realized that each place I go to I am able to bring along just what I need. The hard work of defining oneself, the lessons learned, quite naturally come along with me. I have stories, I have photographs, and I have discovered Instagram.

Presently I am settling into a small apartment in Metz, France with my boyfriend Dany and my daughter Sasha. In addition to the things we use everyday, I have one suitcase full of papers which can probably be better organized into a scrapbook. I am taking a second look at things already sorted and realizing that there are things I can sell which are not serving any purpose in our current lives. Extra wine glasses have a use; we entertain. A print I have no intention of framing and hanging up, probably not.

If my things had once been objects of my ongoing identity construction, perhaps what I hold onto now demonstrates that my identity is in flux. Like stories, we edit life as we go along. The lines, things, which no longer make sense can be let go. I am not afraid of losing parts of my old self. In fact, I actively encourage it.

About Mary Ann Waterman

Mary Ann is originally from Thomaston, Connecticut. Mary Ann has her Bachelor of Arts in English from St. Joseph's University and her Masters in English Literature from Trinity College, with a specialization in metaphysical poetry. She is an Association Montessori International (AMI) trained Montessori educator for 3-6 year old children. Currently, Maryann lives in Metz, France with her nine-year-old daughter. Maryann loves learning new languages, creating recipes, and following a serendipitous life path.

Instagram @ImpracticalLife

Chapter 5

Sovereignty

Gabriela Campos

Sovereignty
Reign
So reign over your entity
To reign over yourself—to rule yourself, your space, your being.

It all starts in your head. Not in a gaslighting, you're imagining things, sort of way...but rather actively reprogramming yourself.

In the following pages, I am going to share with you how I have done this, despite volumes-worth of childhood trauma, abusive relationships, and all the instability that can be associated with all those stories. This is my truth; I hope it can light the path of others so that other people, like yourself, can be free to reign their lives.

To take charge of your mind is to take charge of your life—this is true freedom. I want so much for you, dear reader, to experience this sovereignty. This is real freedom that is not dependent on your circumstances.

It's like anything else, it's hardest to get started. We have societal and familial conditioning, excuses, stories we've made up for ourselves why we can't do this or that—why we are trapped.

There is an image in the Rider Waite tarot deck that exemplifies this. The character's feet are wet, and there's water all around, and perhaps because they are blindfolded they can't know that the water isn't very deep, that it's just a puddle. And, yes, the character is tied to some swords, and perhaps if they were to struggle they might get cut, or feel surrounded by the cold metal blades, but when you explore the image more closely, you will note that they are very loosely bound, as if by a gentle silk ribbon that is barely there. Perhaps that which binds our character might simply fall away if they were to relax and stop struggling, perhaps they would then be able to take the blindfold off and then they could see the way forward.

I have a lot of stories of struggle. I'm certain you do, too. I had a lot of stories in which I was the victim, most people have at least one of those. These stories set up shop in the innermost aspects of my Being...and they had this horrible tendency of repeating themselves. Sometimes the actors were different, and the settings were different, but these stories were like ruts that I could not seem to get out of.

In the Yogic tradition we call these ruts samskaras. They are painful wrong paths so well worn that they become a ditch that one gets stuck in so deeply sometimes that we think it is simply our path, but really the pain and the struggle are trying to tell us, "Wrong way! Change course!" We must learn to look up with ease despite the burdens so we can see our true path.

When I first started realizing that I had the ability to truly be sovereign over my life, I was facing a choice of enduring what was a soul-sucking living hell (that at least afforded me shelter and food) or leaving and essentially becoming homeless with three kids. I had no job, I had given up my career to care for my medically complex, special needs kid and I felt like I couldn't tell a soul what was really happening. A miracle of grace happened when a dear friend asked me how I was—and I actually told the truth. Then another miracle happened. She offered to share her home with me and my three kids—at no charge. Remember the image with the swords? I stopped struggling just long enough for maybe the blindfold to fall down a little. I decided I would not be going back to my then-husband. I couldn't. My children deserved for me not to live out my parents' samskaras.

Here came the first kicker. The father of our three children cleared out our joint bank account without any discussion. He left us without resources, with the intention of leaving me without options. What he did not realize was that I had started to face the truth. The truth does in fact set you free and that is the very first step in reaching sovereignty and true freedom. My truth was that I had choices. I had a safe space to go, and I was ready to own my choice, not allowing myself to be a victim, and facing my truth was freedom.

Whether it's the truth or a lie, it all starts in those few inches between your ears. That little space controls everything in your life, everything you see, feel or hear. It all starts there. Even now, it's all being processed there, in those few inches between your ears. But here's the secret: you're not stuck with whatever your head says. You're not stuck with the programming from your family, your childhood bully, and your ex. Some of those stories are like bad viruses that have been installed into your motherboard. It's corrupted programming, a half-truth meant to throw you for a loop, or rather throw you into a loop—a samskara.

I promise you, you can take the reins over those wild thoughts and pull them out one by one. I'm going to show you how. You will learn how to start dissecting them and understand where they came from. What was their purpose? What was their role? Do those thought forms serve you? If they don't, we must replace them with better programming! You can't just pull them out. Remember the axiom, nature abhors a vacuum. You must replace it. You must put in new programming. I know it sounds too simple to be real, but it's literally how I dug out of the depths of despair.

The first thing I had to do was tell the truth. You and I know we hide behind polite smiles. I tend to really put effort into makeup or my outfit when I'm feeling like I need to show up and "be" something. People had been asking me for years how everything was going, I'd say everything was great. The kids had their struggles, but we were fine. My husband, well, he worked so hard. Half-truths I told myself and the world to conceal the pain and fear.

The truth was that I wasn't OK. Nothing was fine. I was overwhelmed. I felt alone. I felt like nothing I did was ever good enough. I tried so hard. I slept so little. I was on the toddler diet, you know, scarf down what they leave behind on their plate before you wash-the-dishes-diet. I think we have all been there at some point, even if you never had a toddler.

I believe that most of us, if not all of us, have put something else above our basic needs of food, water, sleep, and safety. I was in such a dark place that I just couldn't talk about it, joke about it, or even begin to admit that nothing about my state of being was OK. I was not reigning over my life, I was being pushed, prodded, pulled, and slammed. I was doing it to myself.

I can hear the collective "WHAAAAT?!" from all the corners of all the places that this will be read. I'm sure you're saying to yourself, "but I thought she was describing a soul-sucking experience, at best a deeply dysfunctional marriage. How can she now say that she was doing THIS to herself?!"

Here's where the big leap happens. This is where the soul alchemy takes place that allows us to be free.

I know, I know, how can someone choose this for themselves? Right?

Most, if not all of us, do this on some level, at some point in our lives. We stay in the marriage we're not happy in. We allow behavior towards us at work, at the grocery store, with our families, in school, at a gathering for a romantic partner. We allow microaggressions that grow and grow into very painful and confusing ruts that are in line with the corrupted programing.

This isn't victim blaming. This is me telling you to straighten your crown and take ownership of your kingdom.

Tell the truth. The absolute truth. YOUR absolute truth. Admit to yourself all the things that are bothering you. Let yourself list them—all of them—and then mourn them. Really let all the feelings come up, journal it, draw about it, dance through it —just let it out, be a witness to it. Allow yourself to feel everything.

Let me share one of my recurring patterns that I'm currently working on: My voice/truth/sense of justice.

As a child, I often felt stifled and pushed into neat little boxes that I didn't fit. I was often told that I needed to "pipe down," that I was being too dramatic, that I shouldn't care so much, that I needed to learn to not fight so much. In the background I was being hurt and no one saw it. I'd get in trouble for insisting I had not done things, even though it was true I had not. I wouldn't let myself cry when I was spanked. I'd get in trouble for trying to save caterpillars from the neighborhood boys, or for defending myself when others picked on me.

What was actually happening was that people weren't paying attention when I tried to say things the first few times in softer ways. It seemed that I would only get some movement forward if I pitched a fit. So the only things that were seen were outbursts. I didn't feel supported or safe or heard.

About 40 years into that pattern, I was having the same problem with my children. They couldn't hear me unless I screamed like a banshee. My ex-husband twisted the truth and I started questioning my own sanity and even the idea of truth. I was treated like I was insane because I advocated for my children's health needs. At one of my jobs, I was seen as a threat because I was a truth-teller.

At first glance one might ask, "But what could one do differently?" I was speaking my truth. I was first trying politely, but I was still being labeled as some kind of trouble-maker. Now things are different, and I'm going to tell you the secret for the shift. I changed the words inside of me. I'm not necessarily doing anything big outwardly. It's all happening in that space between the ears. More importantly, I'm linking my thoughts to my heart, really believing them, and projecting them out.

Daily Practice for Sovereignty

Try this as a daily practice. Have a CEO meeting with yourself every morning, or at some point in the day. Don't beat yourself up over it, you're the boss of your life. Sovereignty, remember? The more you are able to put yourself first, first thing, the more you will be able to walk into your day with peace and clear headedness, with true ownership of your day.

You are reigning over your life. You are the boss, the CEO, the Queen or King.

Of course most of us don't live in ashrams or monasteries, nor do we have the luxury of retreats on a daily basis. I'm a single mom with high needs kids. I have to wake up very early and hide, or be very clear about not being disturbed, or even better set things up ahead of time anticipating their needs so that I can meet mine. There will be days when things don't go as planned, and that's ok. Roll with it. Just make sure you take at least 15 minutes for yourself. Just 15 minutes, you can do this!

So what exactly are you supposed to do in these 15 minutes? Here are some ideas to try on, and after a while you will make this time uniquely yours. You are Sovereign.

Set your coffee or tea on a timer if you're not a morning person, so that it will be waiting for you, unless making it mindfully and methodically is part of a waking up process for you.

Take a few moments to stretch in bed. (I have a series that I call bed yoga).

Before your feet hit the ground take three big breaths and take a moment to be grateful for another day, another chance to live out your path, to share your gifts. Maybe take a moment to remind yourself of a few things that you are grateful for, maybe say a prayer, mantra or intention that is relevant to you. I have a Kabbalist Hebrew prayer taped to the sides of my nightstands so that I can remember to say it.

Stand up, get dressed, and go to a place that you have designated for yourself as your quiet place, or have everything next to your bed so that you can do the things before you even stand up for the day.

You can try a few sun-salutations or short Kundalini morning warm ups. You can take the dog for a walk, or just go for a walk. Just find a way to start waking your body up physically. (Walking the dog might take more than 15 minutes; it's just a way to carve out some quiet time for yourself and also get a needed task done.)

Simply sit for a few minutes in stillness. Start with just one minute and build up to what feels necessary. Practice being aware of your breath. Feel it being cool and full of energy as you inhale and observe it taking toxins out of your system as you exhale. Perhaps take the time to meditate on one of your positive sayings/mantras and how it makes you feel, how it might show up in your life.

Maybe you would enjoy pulling a tarot or oracle card from a deck you like. It could be a deck of positive sayings or scriptures. Take big cleansing breaths as you are shuffling, and ask for a message to carry you through the day. Pick a card and meditate on its message for a few minutes, which may mean that you simply sit with it. Maybe you leave the card in a place you will see a lot. I like having things above the kitchen sink. Maybe you have a notebook you use all day and you have a clear plastic sleeve that you can stick it into, or maybe take a picture of it. Maybe it inspires you to draw or write for a few minutes. Maybe it inspires you to send a note of love and gratitude to a loved one or someone you haven't connected with for some time.

Once you've done your practice either from the things above, or whatever else you would like to try, enjoy your coffee or tea or whatever you enjoy drinking in the morning and look at your to-dos for the day. Now you can hit the ground running with clarity and peace, fully in charge of your head space—true sovereignty.

External shifts will start happening around you because you choose to create a beautiful internal vortex of love and positivity. The shift starts with you, then it spreads to your bedroom, your bathroom, your kitchen, your living room. The concentric circles start moving outward.

After my divorce, life reconfigured in such a way that I moved back into the home I had shared with my husband. When I first moved back into my home, I refused to sleep in my room until I repainted the walls. For me that was a way for me to change the energy of the room, to imbue it with love and light.

To start a new chapter, I became very intentional on what I would allow in my room. I started making my bed daily. I got rid of clutter and clothes that I didn't wear anymore. Instead of it happening from a chore mentality, I did everything as an act of radical self-love. I love myself enough that it matters. This is my kingdom, I'm in charge of myself and my surroundings. There were no excuses, no storiesYou are Sovereign. just that it mattered to me, and so I made it happen. Even if it happened a little at a time, I just kept working on it.

Now I'm working on my yard. I always wanted to have chickens and grow fruit trees, but that wasn't permitted under the previous reign. I got the chickens and I built them a coop and a run. This is now my third flock and third iteration. For the past two seasons, I have been purchasing perennial native food plants. The idea of planting and replanting a garden every year just didn't make sense to me. I'm making a food forest because that's sovereignty for me. It allows me a certain freedom from the System because I am choosing to make my own. I'll still be planting annuals—some perhaps a little less usual, but the thought of it all makes me happy so I go with it.

Maybe you start owning your space differently. Maybe for you it's creating a peaceful spot under a tree where you can recharge, read a book or a magazine after work. Maybe it's creating a spot for your CEO morning meeting with yourself. What you create and make space for is going to change over time and that's OK; just keep making space for yourself in your own little kingdom.

You will notice that your words start changing and your relationships start changing, too. As you become fully honest with yourself, you will find that you no longer have patience for people's veneer. Some people will appreciate being truly seen, while others will be horrified at feeling unmasked simply by you living your truth. That's OK. You have to be true to yourself.

Be truthful with yourself, be kind with yourself, and allow only what is necessary. As we reign in our brains, we reign in our actions and our speech. Eventually the people around you will mirror this. Change is hard. It won't come without some challenges and pain, but as all the knots unravel, you see yourself free from the bonds of negative patterns that were holding you back, how you walk in the world will start to change.

I choose to walk in places as sovereign and I'm treated accordingly—as I like to say in my yoga classes, "don't let your crown fall."

About Gabriela Campos

Gabriela descends from healers, intuitives, and trouble-makers from all over the globe. She was born in Peru and although she moved to the United States while she was still young, her patterns had already been formed. Duality and its quantum dance are how she has been able to survive and thrive even in circumstances many couldn't imagine. This has given her the gift to naturally look at the world from multiple perspectives. This gift along with her insatiable desire for knowledge, sprinkled with her intuitive abilities, makes her a sought after advisor, teacher, and healer.

Gabriela is a momma, energy healer, nascent herbalist, yoga teacher, tarot and oracle reader, artist, advocate, urban farmer, and a lover of life. She has had to work hard at rebuilding her own life through multiple challenges and loves helping others find a way forward. As she likes to say in classes, "As we all heal ourselves, we spread infinite ripples of light that touch others. We don't know how many other people their light ripples will also impact. May you be light."

IG: Ella_gabriela_delatierra

Email: ella.gabriela.delatierra@gmail.com

Clearing Clutter

Rosemary King

"I will put the pieces back together, and my foundation will be stronger than it was before. Vive ut vivas. Live that you may live."

Rachel Schemmerling

"Biologically, we don't need much. A roof over our heads, clothing, food. How is it that, as a society, a culture has developed that makes us want more? And more, and more."

JaneSTORM

"I find when I am stressed, my go-to is water or nature. This helps me weed my mind garden. Each day, I go out with a purpose to look up, look around, and look ahead."

Janet Johnson

"To me, this is what embracing your space means. It's turning a house into your home. Each room should serve its purpose, outside of storing random stuff. Each room should have something that catches your eye and makes you smile."

Sheri Giancarlo

"We come into this world with nothing and leave with nothing. What happens in between is living; living in space, surrounded by stuff that in the end loses its identity when it meets the fate of a dumpster."

Chapter 6

To be Clutter-Free is to be Healed from Within

Rosemary King

The path to healing is usually unexpected. Sometimes you don't realize you're healing until you're in the middle of it. I've noticed that when there is physical clutter around me, it is an extension of the emotional chaos I've been clinging to since childhood. I've healed parts of my past, yet there has always been another trauma around the corner; one that holds me down beneath the water, as if I'm drowning. The emotional clutter I hold onto continues to burden me as much as the physical clutter that I cannot release. I've learned that it is a continual process for someone who hasn't fully healed from past trauma or does not have a healthy self-relationship.

As a child, my mom did the best she could, raising five daughters, working, volunteering, and battling chronic illnesses. There was constant fighting and instability for my entire childhood, and as a result, there was always clutter and no good guidance on how to best tackle it in our home. Even with our best intentions to keep things tidy, clutter accumulated.

When I was a teen, I didn't have to share a room, but I didn't understand how to keep it organized. It would take me two days to clean out the clutter and trash from my space and within a week it would be right back to the mess it was before.

Sometimes I would catch my mom pulling the stuff I was throwing away out of the garbage and saving it for me. She would tell me that she was keeping it because I might need it one day. Why throw away something unbroken or in good condition? In her mind, there was no reason for it to be in the trash. I remember having to wait for my mom to be out of the house or not paying attention so I could throw things away outside in the trash can rather than in the kitchen to prevent her from digging through everything.

In my early childhood, I had an affinity for the occult and challenged church teachings. This was not done out of disrespect, but out of honest curiosity. How could the church say lying was a sin or hurting people was a sin, but to speak the truth was a punishment? These contradictions made me want to pursue other ways to understand God and what it meant to be loved and to love unconditionally.

My quest for something greater eventually took over, and I left the church many years ago, never regretting nor looking back. I realized that forced obedience could no longer tie me down, and I no longer accepted the notion that if I weren't obedient, then I wasn't worthy of love. In my twenties and into my thirties, these lessons were a part of my life, and during those periods of reflection, I experienced peace in my mind, body, spirit, and physical spaces.

I believe my journey began before childhood. Ancestral patterns follow us, and I believe that these patterns, for better or worse, can be changed or broken and replaced with something better by current living generations. However, as a child, I only knew what I knew.

For me, I never knew a happy childhood or what a home without chaos looked like. I experienced many traumas. As an adult, I took the Adverse Childhood Experiences (ACEs) screening and scored an 8/10. The ACEs screening showed how much abuse, neglect, and household challenges a child endures before their 18th birthday. Many people may experience one or two of these without issue. But those that score a four or above, these experiences start to impact their health and well-being.

As I reflect, I can see how my perspective shifted. I went from feeling like I was being punished for things I didn't do to understanding I could control the outcomes of my struggles by taking ownership of my thoughts, deeds, and actions. When there is self-love in my life and it flows freely without conditions, life feels better. When there is a blockage of love, there is a blockage of inspired action leading to inaction and frustration.

As a child, I learned that love was conditional. There were terms to adhere to, and if you didn't, then "love" wasn't given. I realize now that this warped idea of love was rooted in someone else's belief that they wanted to accept "love" in their lives. This "love" usually required blind obedience, following their needs, and anything deviating from that was wrong.

I didn't realize that all the clutter around me in my personal space was a manifestation of the emotional baggage I was holding onto inside. Seeing chaos from my parents also played a role in my habits, but deep down, it was the trauma that I was and still am carrying around that is a contributing factor to the clutter in my life. But it's not without trying. It's the persistence that catches me every time. Consistency is vital in my experience, and it is through steady work the most significant leaps of faith can lead me to a whole new world of enlightenment and understanding.

I was constantly sick as a child, and it was no wonder. My illness took a nose-dive as I got older and started a family of my own. I continued with the same habits I had always known. Life wasn't too bad when there was one kid, but eight years and six kids later, well, you can probably imagine what my house resembled.

Life was more than chaotic; it was darn-right suffocating at times. Unable to breathe and walking on eggshells to keep the peace, I eventually gave up on an organized house, one that would be spotless and magazine-worthy, because I couldn't cope. I did try my best to be satisfied with knowing that I spent time with my kids, volunteered in the community, and gave of myself in ways that contributed to a better life for my children.

I remember there were days in my twenties when all I could do was get out of bed, feed the kids, and go to sleep on the couch. Nothing else got done; not the dishes, laundry, or anything of importance. I let the kids have free range because I was too sick to do anything. I spent many years trying to prove my worth and usefulness in the world because I felt inadequate as a mom in my community. Throughout it all, I neglected myself to the point of complete exhaustion.

After ten years of not knowing what was physically wrong with me, I finally had my answers. I had a primary immune deficiency called Common Variable Immune Deficiency. I now receive infusions to replace what my body doesn't make artificially. However, my illness has also been a blessing in disguise. It has given my kids more empathy and caring hearts. They are generous with their time and find ways to help others as often as they can.

I didn't connect trauma wounds and clutter until I was much older, and it was staring me in the face. Reflecting on my life, I can see how much I clung to the physical clutter to mask my emotional pain. I didn't make the direct connection to my healing from trauma until I repeated that process. As time went on, I grew as a person, and my living space and physical environment had times of upgrades as well.

I'm not proud of all the choices I've made, but I'm learning that forgiveness toward myself helps remove the burden I'm holding onto within me. I started to look at life through a new lens and challenged myself to learn what I could do to improve my health. For me, the answer was to heal from all of my trauma.

Healing from trauma isn't easy; I have to peel back the layers of each event that happened, how and why it happened, and the aftermath of it all. Sometimes I am unable to finish and have had to stop because I cannot rush this process.

If I pushed or rushed too quickly, I would ultimately find myself back to where I was before starting. When I took the time to heal, I examined the finer details, even the painful ones, and moved forward. When I had a breakthrough with my healing, clearing out clutter came naturally and with a tenacity that I don't see in myself often.

In 2012 I learned the art of Reiki and applied it to my life for further healing. It opened doors that I never knew existed and permitted me to see my life in a new and better way truly. I found that all was not lost and that I could find my way back to being in touch with the Divine. I let go of the layers of myself that were no longer serving a purpose for me.

At that point in my life, I began to understand how my emotions played a role in me holding onto physical clutter. Unfortunately, like all things, when I stopped, the chaos returned with a vengeance. My emotional self was sabotaging my efforts again.

The strides I've made and the times I've fallen have a direct link to challenges I've had to endure. It is not only the physical and emotional clutter; it is also the feeling of failing myself and my kids every time I hit another wall in staying on top of the chaos around me.

Even so, I keep plugging away. Picking up the broken pieces of myself, the shattered pieces of my life, and pushing through the pain and sorrow to put myself back together. Up and down, this cycle continues at some level even today.

Over the next few years, I focused on working through my shadow-self while continuing to release parts of my past that no longer bring me joy or pleasure. I continue down this path to this day. Tackling the hard stuff doesn't come naturally, so I took smaller steps to tackle my life and gave myself grace throughout the process.

When I first started to focus on the clutter around me, I spent time meditating and going deep within to learn more about myself and my thoughts and feelings surrounding the things I was passively clutching. It turns out most of the things I kept, I did so because I didn't want to hurt someone's feelings, even though many times that person was no longer part of my life. Funny how that works.

I would start with the energy around me - opening windows, smudging the room I was working in, listening to music, or using other techniques to remove any negative energy from my living space before tackling the clutter. It boosted my energy and allowed me to clean for much more extended periods than trying to clean from a place of dread. Mindset and persistence were the key.

When I was ready to tackle a room, I would spend my time assessing the space and what was mostly under control already and improve it. Then I would move on to the more challenging places. It took time and practice, and like any reasonable person, I fell off the wagon but remembered to pick myself up again.

Sometimes, if I felt defeated over the amount of time and energy, I would need to remove clutter from a room, starting with one bag. One bag, whether trash or clutter, out of the house. Super easy. Then came another bag, then another, until I was able to get into a rhythm and breeze through a room. Sometimes, one bag was all I could complete. And that was okay too.

One bag might not seem like much, but those small wins pushed me out of my comfort zone, like stretching. When you haven't reached for your toes in a few years, you struggle, but give it a few days or maybe weeks, and after, you eventually reach your toes or at least reach further than you could before without the practice. Removing clutter is a lot like that; it takes hard work to remove and keep clutter out of your life.

Maintaining that one bag-a-day mindset prevented overwhelm from creeping up and offered a long-term solution to removing clutter from my home. It's simple enough that it isn't going to take up too much time, but also something I can do year-round.

Removing clutter may bring up some challenging emotions that you've hidden away. Who knew that going through your childhood toys would stir up feelings of inadequacy, failure, or disappointment? Some things in your possession might bring on thoughts of happiness and joy! Those are the things that may make you pause before casually giving them away.

I spent 2017-2018 doing deep healing around my childhood when I took a leap of faith and spent nine months in a public speaking Mastermind. Those nine months allowed me the safe space for free expression without judgment, anger, or hate. It was a place where I could go without feeling I was alone on my journey. I gained more courage and support during that time than at any point in my life, and for that experience, I am forever grateful.

The struggle was to keep going on the days that I wanted to quit; too much pain coursing through my body, sleepless nights, and waking up in a panic. At times I felt suffocated in the emotions and clutter surrounding me.

After the Mastermind completed, I found myself again on a beautiful path of inspired growth and expansion. I continued removing the physical clutter around me to share my story with others. I spoke at the Empowered Light Expo on the topic of Forgiveness and Health in Oaks, Pennsylvania. I was a featured contributor to *Breaking the Silence Summit: Healing Childhood Sexual Trauma*.

Before our final move to Connecticut in the fall of 2019, I remember placing a piece of my past where I first expressed my childhood depression. Glued to a pink piece of construction paper and decorated with multi-colored balloons, I wrote, "Wouldn't it be..." I distinctly remember my teacher asking me why I didn't write about something happy, but there was nothing I could identify as happiness in my life.

As I begin life in my forties, I am learning to work with myself gently, offering myself grace and latitude for the struggles I've endured and the demons that still haunt my nights. I look forward to the day when the internal monsters are no longer by my side tormenting me.

Today, I can feel the power struggle of what I need to do to improve my physical, emotional, and spiritual spaces. Voicing my trauma has always been challenging because there is fear, shame, and humiliation accompanying my desire to share with my desire to keep it within me.

Sharing my struggles, pain, and discomfort gives me comfort in knowing that my story may help others find their voice.

When I get to the other side of these personal struggles, all I've learned will still be with me, guiding me, and I will easily be able to rebuild where the foundation crumbled beneath my feet. I will put the pieces back together, and my foundation will be stronger than it was before.

"Vive ut vivas."

Live that you may live.

About Rosemary King

Rosemary King is the owner of Heart-Led Concierge, a personal assistant service provider in Northeastern Connecticut. She offers home management, personal care management, decluttering and organizing, and other services to support families and small businesses. Heart-Led Concierge was created out of the need to spread love and compassion to moms with chronic illnesses. In 2009, Rosemary was diagnosed with a rare immune deficiency. As a result of her condition, she recognizes the challenges families like hers face when they're too sick to meet those needs.

In addition to growing her business, she currently volunteers at the Navy-Marine Corps Relief Society and is a member of Soroptimist International of Willimantic. Rosemary is also a Justice of the Peace in the town where she lives with her large family. Rosemary earned her bachelor's degree in Psychology and a certification as a birth and bereavement doula.

She is married to Wayne and they have six children, ages 12-21 years. Her family enjoys hiking, camping, and antiquing together. They also have a German Shepherd and pet ferret. Rosemary has been featured on popular sites such as Thrive Global, Medium, The Mighty, Realtor.com, and others. Fun fact, she was a makeover participant on the hit TV show, *What Not to Wear.* Her episode *Homecoming* is streaming on TLC.

www.heartledconcierge.com
support@heartledconcierge.com
Facebook @Heartledconcierge

Chapter 7

Letting Go:
Our Relationship with Stuff

Rachel Schemmerling

The national obsession with clutter and decluttering seems relatively recent. It pops up daily on social media, print publications, TV shows, and it has even become a profession. To me, however, it's always been there: growing up with a family that loved collecting, then working with my clients' clutter, then focusing on my own need to keep things organized. I like to joke that it's part of my DNA, and I realized very early that the relationship between people and their stuff is very human and tends to be very emotional.

Family Clutter and the Feelings that Go with It

I grew up in a home with parents that loved stuff. Not hoarders, but let's just say "collectors." Of everything!

My mother is a gifted artist, cook, and writer who is compassionate, full of life, and loved by everyone. She's embraced her Native American and French Canadian genealogy and culture, and authored books on Native American cooking, culture, and lore. She began to show signs of dementia in recent years which has made organization both distracting and overwhelming. She built a wall around her office area made of paper and books. Her office would fill up with piles of new plastic bins to attempt to get "organized" again. She grew up with limited means so a filled pantry meant security. It didn't matter if she already had two cans of something, if it was on sale and she'd already used one, she would purchase a few more. Even food can be clutter.

My father has unique and varied interests. His passions, like many of his possessions, reveal his love of the past. He's a craftsman, a historic home lover, vintage car enthusiast, a historian and Revolutionary War reenactor, and he loves a good story. He's wise and self-educated, but if given the opportunity for a college degree he would likely have a PhD in several topics. Like my mother, he is interested in our family's Revolutionary War ancestors and our genealogy. Influenced by a childhood during the frugal World War II years, he still has collections of large metal bins because "you never know when you might need that part."

Both of my parents are now elderly. My siblings and I look ahead and wonder how we are going to dismantle eight decades of stuff. How do you sort it out? Where will it go? Who wants all of this? Who has room? Which things will mean so much to one of us, but may mean nothing to another? Will any of it matter?

And that's just the logistics. Next comes the emotion and the guilt. Will we argue over things that bring us warm memories? Or will we callously toss them aside? Will we fight over who is getting which Christmas ornament or what valuable bowl? Will I ask myself, *"if it meant a lot to my mother, does that mean I'm required to keep it?"* I am certain it will be an experience like no other in our lives.

My relationship with furnishings and collections plus my sense of home and overall space has stayed with me from childhood to adulthood and influenced me both personally and professionally.

The Energy Belongings Hold and How It Affects Us

About 10 years ago, I opened a home furnishings consignment store. I had more than 200 consignors bringing in collectibles, furniture, and decorative accessories all within two months of opening. It was then I started to understand how "things" hold energy. I felt the consignors were also projecting emotional energy about their stuff. Sure, many were unwanted items. Sometimes, however, the consignors wanted to keep them, but had to downsize or they needed money.

It wasn't always about the money. Most consignors just wanted to know their items were going to someone that would use them and become part of their homes. I would make them laugh and say that our shop was like an adoption agency where furniture and other items are carefully placed into the right hands. Owning this shop wasn't just about the joy I had in styling the displays and selling great merchandise. These experiences taught me that things or belongings—and people—hold energy. I started to sense good and bad energy from things. It was also during the first year that I owned my shop that my health began to deteriorate.

By nature I am an empath. And I can easily and deeply sense the feelings of others. I started to feel the energy of these items, and it began to affect my overall health. Who knows, maybe I'm dreaming up a conspiracy theory but it was a great lesson. I began to look at things differently. Even items in my own home. A friend that had deeply broken my trust had given me a set of dishes, and every time I picked up those dishes, I felt ill. It was not only a reminder of the person and the experience, I literally felt sick. I removed those dishes from my home...and voila! Problem solved. I strongly believe in the importance of removing items like this from your home that might be causing negative energy or simply adding clutter to your life.

Walking Away from it All and Letting Go

Apparently, I was not the only one who thought this. Instead of my helping clients come to terms with decluttering, a friend and client taught ME a lesson.

She looked at me and said, "Well, take whatever you want."

I was dumbfounded. I thought, "Wait, what do you mean, 'take whatever I want?'"

All of her family's belongings were piled up on the living room floor awaiting removal. All the belongings were there to either be taken or given away. Much of it had already sold at a tag sale and some was donated to local charities.

It had only been a year and half. We had just worked together for several months to choose paint colors, window treatments, and furniture layout. I met them at my daughter's preschool; our daughters were friends. We also became good friends, and they asked me to help them design their new home.

But now, they were selling the house and moving to France with only the items they could carry on their backs or those that could be easily packed.

I initially thought about all the time and effort we put into the house 18 months earlier; was that time wasted? Then I was in awe of how anyone could just walk away from all their personal belongings including books, kitchen items, clothing, and furniture. I was deeply and emotionally affected by the thought of "how do we let go?" What is the reason behind our relationship with "things"? Are we that materialistic? Biologically, we don't need much. A roof over our heads, clothing, and food. How is it that, as a society, a culture has developed that makes us want more? And more, and more.

As an interior designer, I'm technically a professional shopper. I carefully source and curate the proper items to fill a home that solves a problem and supports the occupants' activities and lives. I accessorize and create environments filled with things. I began to wonder, from this perspective, when we look at "things" and ask, do we really need it all? Or how can we begin to do without so many possessions?

How do you do that? I had to really think about that and realize how incredibly connected we can be to our possessions. It forced me to take a hard look at my own things, and to let go of some.

This need (or is it really "want"?) for stuff has most homes bursting at the seams. We have tag sales and consign or donate to get rid of some stuff and then turn around and bring other stuff home. I realized that when things accumulate without a plan or intention, I get very anxious. And it made me look into how clutter affects people in different ways.

I'm not a minimalist by any means. However, that view certainly has its benefits. It might be good to really think hard before making a purchase and living with good quality items that are useful, functional, and meaningful. My personal and professional experiences have revealed that I DO believe in letting go of the excess while enjoying and cherishing what I choose to keep.

About Rachel Schemmerling

Rachel's love for design began at an early age—both by nature and by nurture. She grew up in a 275-year-old Colonial farmhouse in coastal Connecticut which gave her a first look into the world of home design that was to become her passion. She now works with busy families to design an eco-friendly, serene, and healthy home that allows for functionality, sense of place, and peace of mind.

It took a personal chronic diagnosis for Rachel to learn more about the benefits of a slower lifestyle and how to incorporate wellness-focus with interior designing. It was her need for happiness in her surroundings that became vital for her health journey as well. Rachel credits her supportive family and the serenity and comfort of her home in helping to manage her overall wellbeing. On a professional level, she's gained a unique understanding about how craving calm, comforting home environments can also improve one's health.

She holds a Bachelor of Art degree in Interior Design and a degree in Hospitality Management from the University of New Haven and a certification by the Wellness Within Your Walls educational program. A strong believer in the importance of historic preservation, she was an Executive Co-Chair of a two-year fundraising effort to restore the 200-year-old Congregational Church in Killingworth, Connecticut and serves as Secretary on a Historic Review Committee.

Rachel feels blessed with a wonderfully supportive husband, son, and daughter, and she derives much joy from her dogs, Snuggles and Ginger. She is grateful to do what she loves and takes pride in her ability to design with empathy, heart, with an ever-acute eye on wellness.

www.timelesslivingdesigns.com

Chapter 8

Clearing Mind Clutter

JaneSTORM

My mom says I came out of the womb collecting people, things, and ideas. It has taken me 56 years to set up positive boundaries to curate my collections. In 2021, I am coaching people to Clear their Mind Clutter. As "they" say, we teach what we need to learn.

I have given some thought to why I am considered a collector. I think it all began with curiosity and commitment to others. I love people and finding out how they tick. I love things, and I have a visceral reaction to items and information.

Three years ago, my sister invited me to a retreat in her home. She took us through a vision board exercise. She started with a poem titled *Where I'm From* by George Ella Lyon. Here is my version as a way of introduction.

Where I am From

I am Jane.
I am a Gemini.
I am from the suburbs.
I am from a world filled with colorful characters.
I am in a place where I always knew I was loved.
I am from groups of women, from childhood, college, England, Verizon, Yorktown, Relay and beyond.
I am an explorer of emotions, of things, of places.
I am from a loving, safe, wonderful marriage.

I am from a loud, fun, soul singing, dance party family filled with love, expectations, hidden fears, happy times, giving spirits, strong hearts, loud voices, and some soft voices that are getting stronger.

I am from a creative, colorful, character-based series of connections.

I am from happy.

I am from sunshine.

I am from bumps in the road where I have picked myself up.

I am from birds singing, sharing food with squirrels.

I am from stars twinkling and shining bright.

I am from Hope, Love, PurplePower and Passion.

I am from a strong work ethic filled with flexibility, fierceness, and fun with 31 phenomenal years of connecting and surviving in Corporate America and achieving all that I have wanted.

I am from taking risks and learning daily.

I am from networking in person as well as virtually.

I am from Transformational Coaching, co-creating life changes through mind mapping and affirmations.

I am surrounded by people and things who connect me with Happy.

I am from love.

This poem got me thinking. How can I honor who I am and move forward with less clutter? Why is clutter a trigger for me? How can I support others in Clearing their Mind Clutter? Here is my journey.

Contributor to Clutter

"The greatest need of our time is to clean out the enormous mass of mental and emotional rubbish that clutters our minds." - Thomas Merton

I have realized that so many of us overthink. We have expectations and assumptions of how things are "supposed to be" and those thoughts clog our brain waves. It takes a ton of energy to overthink. It takes time away from productivity. It affects sleep and creates a barrier for success.

The first sign that things are stressful in my life is the armchair in my bedroom begins overflowing with clothes. That *chair* represents the guts of me; the side that doesn't have it all together; the side that has too much stuff; the side that gets lazy about putting things back where they belong; the side of me that changes four or five times before I go out to an event because I am not loving my weight at the moment; and the side that shows truly the controlled chaos of my life. I work hard every day to do my best, yet I cannot ever get my chair to be clothing free for more than a week at a time!

When stress hits, my chair pile gets higher, and waking up at 3:21 am begins. There are pages and pages I've written in a journal about finances, worthiness, parenting, passion projects, future endeavors, expectations, striving to stay in my own lane yet wanting to help friends and family with health and personal issues, and trying not to let others down. You get the idea.

Truth be told, socks are the bane of my existence! There are so many damn socks on that chair that have lost their mate, and I am beyond rescuing them! So I get up every day with an intention to get it all together and life happens and there is a realization that perfection is hard to achieve and that is OK.

There are those of you who are reading this and can relate to my chair, and others whose OCD and neatness meters are going haywire. (I bet you are ready to come rescue my chair and me!) There is shame in clutter. There is judgment in clutter. There is pride and ego and anxiety in clutter. Clutter puts people on the defense. I believe there is power in mind-cluttered over-thinkers sharing their version of the chair more often. When we get down to it, having the courage to name the clutter and to trust in the process of understanding why it is in our lives gave me the power to begin my journey into Clearing Mind Clutter.

When I think of mind and physical clutter, I think of stuff. This led me to looking up the definition of "stuff" in the Merriam Webster Dictionary. The part of the definition that stood out most for me was: *"filling an object or your mind with stuff so that there is no room for anything else.*" How many times have you said after Thanksgiving dinner, "I am so stuffed and I need to lay down"? That visual is a billboard in my mind. I keep saying, 'Jane, why do you need so much stuff in your head and your space?' It makes me tired thinking about it! It is like caffeine for me. At first, it is a jolt of energy but later it comes crashing down.

Creative Choices

When we think about mind clutter, there are choices we can make. We can surrender to it or we can define it, delve into it and practice discipline by creating habits to move forward. As a Certified Transformational Coach, I am creating accountability by exploring The Wheel of Life. I am supporting life-changing motivation and sustainable achievement by exploring possibilities and insights in these elements of my clients' lives: personal, health, lifestyle, relationships, career, and finances. This not only supports my clients but has turned a mirror on me.

When my kids were little and rambunctious, my mom would say, "Get them in the bath or get them outside." This advice worked not only for my kids but for me, too. I find when I am stressed, my go-to is water or nature. This helps me weed my mind garden. Each day, I go out with a purpose to look up, look around, and look ahead.

In December 2018, I left Corporate America after spending my entire adult life working at Verizon. I loved my job and did not expect to leave but got an offer that could not be refused. I had 30 days to act. I ran the loyalty program for business-to-business customers. My program, Small Biz Rewards, was my third child. I was an evangelist for loyalty and fought for the program every single day I managed it. I was a trailblazer when it came to remote work and job sharing. I now recognize that this arrangement encouraged me to keep my mind and physical clutter clear at that time. I created a successful virtual career long before the COVID-19 pandemic. I managed a cross functional team of people in all different states, I shared a job for 15 years where I worked in

NY Monday through Wednesday and my job share partner worked in Virginia Wednesday through Friday. We were known as a "well-oiled machine."

In the Fall of 2018, I could see that things were shifting at Verizon. My mind was cluttered. I was overthinking the future. I was not sure what was going to happen to my program. If they shut it down, I would be on the defensive for many months for my loyalty vendors that managed all the day-to-day activities and for the loyal customers. I would grieve the loss of my "Happy Place" at Verizon. I also knew that I am much better on offense than defense. I decided to take the leap, to go out on my own terms while still having a fondness for loyalty to pursue other opportunities that drove my passion. I believed that being given generous severance pay and benefits was too rich to pass up and would probably not be offered again. I volunteered to leave in October 2018. I was off the payroll on December 31, 2018.

I distinctly remember being on a business trip after I made the decision, driving from one call center to another. I was thinking, 'OK Jane, you are leaving Verizon, the place you have called home for your entire adult life, what the heck are you going to do?'

I had worked for years with our loyalty vendor, Kobie Marketing. One day in 2016, I showed up for a meeting at their headquarters and they had a huge sign hanging in their creative department and it said JaneSTORM. It stopped me in my tracks and I turned to them and asked about the sign. They said, "When you come to town, we don't brainstorm, we JaneSTORM. You connect people with ideas better than anyone else we know." At that moment, alone in the car, it came to me. I said it out loud, I am going to have a company called JaneSTORM and it is going to connect people with ideas. Looking back, it is clear that my trailblazing role at Verizon set my foundation to have rules for mind clutter and to move forward.

This started me on a journey that I never expected to have. I distinctly remember saying to my boss at my review four years ago when asked what new learning I wanted, "I don't want to learn anything new. I am happy and content with where I am." Fast forward three years and I am learning something new and meeting new people every single day. My curiosity has opened my brain to so many possibilities. I am taking time to embrace the new sensations in life with the willingness to expand my horizons.

At the same time, I am working hard on feeding my subconscious mind with affirmations. The affirmations support my confidence and clarity. They are written with intention and are brief, precise, positive, and present tense. Affirmation statements are successful when they are believed, displayed, and repeated. It is enlightening to witness my positive conscious choices come alive from affirmations being fed to my subconscious mind. The affirmations are backed up by action, repetition and a plan and purpose to take charge. Each day, those affirmations guide me in my endeavor to get to the heart of the clutter.

I recently read that 75% of our thoughts are the same thoughts as the day before. Wow! That hit me. I am working on creating a new self-sustaining garden in my mind by weeding it daily. There are two mantras that have served me well personally and as a Certified Transformational Coach. The first is, "Stay in your own lane, Jane." This mantra has made me realize it is totally acceptable to be kind and firm with boundaries at the same time. It is empowering to focus on the commitment I made for myself and getting others to respect the boundaries that I have established.

Stay in Your Own Lane means:

- Stop comparing myself and my journey to others.
- Staying out of other people's business.
- Staying in openness about other choices even if I do not agree with them.
- Letting go of ego, expectations, and assumptions.
- Speaking my truth without fear of repercussions.
- Being true to me.
- Letting go of the "fixer" mindset.

- Knowing what I am good at and where I need support in business and life.

The second mantra that has sustained me in 2020 and 2021 is "Just Listen, Jane." Before I was a coach, many of my relationships were based on giving advice. Now, there is curiosity, lots of powerful, open-ended questions, and holding space to listen. It comes down to attitude. When we come to a situation with the intent to listen and to notice patterns and leave our expectations at the door, we open our mind space to unlimited possibilities. When I find myself jumping to conclusions or judgments, I now stop and ask myself, "I wonder what is going on for them?" This practice opens the conversation to different options. My commitment to a couple of creative mantras has created a space for clear, honest, and accepting communication in my personal and professional relationships.

Sometimes, it is our circumstances that are the catalyst for change. In December 2020, my mom was diagnosed with a rare and aggressive form of uterine cancer. Holy Cow! Let us talk about the amount of mind clutter invading my mind since the diagnosis! There has been a roller coaster of thoughts, questions, and fears in my mind at different times. We have lived through a failed surgery, two more surgeries, an aggressive cancer diagnosis and many doctor appointments all during a pandemic while many states away from our immediate family. This has been when I have had to coach myself, empowering myself to stay in the present moment, trusting the process.

I heard a quote from Brother Richard Hendrick on an Instagram live last year that resonated with me, "Fears decrease the minute we name them." Taking time to name my fears in a journal or with my trust team has given me the space to explore how I am feeling, what is in my control, what I must send out to the universe, and hope for the best outcome possible. I am trying to take my cues from Mom instead of my cluttered mind. She looks great, feels good, has a positive attitude and outlook. It is so strange to her that at 85 she can look and feel as good as she does.

She does not own her cancer. She is teaching many of us about patience and living in the present moment.

My mother has four children. Three daughters and a son. We are each bringing our super powers to the table. My power is building community, powerful questioning of people in charge, and kick ass note taking. My brother's is storytelling and an unending amount of inspirational knowledge. My eldest sister took on the physical clutter and cleared mom's physical space for 30 days straight. I keep saying I missed the "Marie Kondo" gene and she got an abundance of it. My other sister brought her baking and gardening skills to the table. Each of us is working on clearing our minds as best as possible to be present during this time. We meet each Sunday on Zoom and we are working on having our minds clutter free when it comes to the support we are giving to our mom. I am practicing letting go of assumptions and expectations, some days minute by minute. The space of the unknown causes anxiety, and witnessing a loved one go through the roller coaster of healing has instigated an immediate need to look closely at my daily practices and how I want to show up in this world. So, yes, the universe has a sense of humor and a lesson book for each one of us.

Creating Space

"When you throw out the physical clutter, we clear our minds. When we throw out the mental clutter, we clear our souls." - Gail Blanke

My husband is an only child. His father recently had to move from the apartment he lived in for 56 years. My husband's life until the age of 21 was locked up in that apartment. His bedroom was frozen in time for 34 years. As his spouse, it was important to allow him to grieve as he sorted through his feelings and his "clutter." He and I recently discussed how we assign values to items and how we honor the people and the value assigned. His parents believed in continuity - once you buy something high quality, you keep it. They believed in the theory you had what you used and used what you had. Their bedroom, dining room and living room sets were owned since 1966; his parents never thought of getting new furniture. His mom had many losses in her life, and my husband believes she kept the furniture because it gave her control as opposed to many other things in her life. They did not have a ton of clutter, but they had stuff accumulated that still had to be taken care of in 2019.

Watching him process the memories made us think about our own house and how we have attached value to our infinite number of prized possessions. During the pandemic, it was clear that stuff had taken on a different meaning for us. We realized how little we need, yet our minds are having a hard time letting go.

Recently, we came up with a three-year plan to become snowbirds. This is exciting and terrifying. Our big house is full of 22 years of accumulated stuff. We have lived there for 23 years but one silver lining of the pandemic is in the past year, we did not add to our collection and one of our kids has moved out, so we are down a tiny bit in the "stuff" category. We have spent hours in our minds justifying the contents in our home.

My husband has been in our home in New York while I have been in Florida as my mom's caregiver for the past four months. We Facetime regularly. Recently he had the bright idea to clean out our mudroom. He found 64 pairs of shoes and 46 coats! There were only three people in our house! He Facetimed me with excitement, and then we had a fight. I did not want to let go of any shoes or coats! I hung up on him. I was crying while driving. I pulled over and took a pause. *Why was this upsetting me so much? What had I learned about stuff in the past year? What was I holding on to? How was I going to move past this hurdle if I genuinely want to become a snowbird in three years?*

I waited an hour and called him back. We set a date for that night to try again. This time our conversation was interactive. I sang "Let It Go" to him, we laughed, and we got through my kryptonite first: my shoes! He had the mandatory three piles: Keep, Toss, Donate. It took less than 20 minutes. I sipped my wine and went in for more. The coats took longer. I kept thinking, "I like that one so much." Truth is, I felt like I was giving away some old friends. I know I do not need seven black coats, but I wanted them. It finally came down to me realizing I could give them to someone who needed them way more than I do. Giving them away will bring someone else joy and contribute to my growth of clearing my physical and mental clutter. I needed to set a firm goal. I needed a disinterested party who was a catalyst to get things moved. I am giving myself time to enjoy, reflect, let go, and cherish the memories. We are taking photos, writing vignettes, laughing at some of the crap that has been saved for years and wondering why it is so hard to let go.

This all has led me to where I am today. Teaching what I need to learn. Focusing on clearing my mind-clutter and supporting others for the purpose of creating positive thought patterns that fill the mind with passion, priorities, and purposeful action. Mind-clutter can be positive. When I think of others with cluttered minds, I believe that they are creative, understanding, fun, spontaneous, empathetic, and hopeful. I am working with myself and my clients to discover patterns, to recognize the details, and to detach the negative from the positive in order to activate positive thoughts, to clear space for a flourished mind garden of clarity, and to create positive and forward-thinking transformation in the mental and physical spaces of life.

About JaneSTORM

JaneSTORM (aka Jane McCarthy) is a Certified Master Coach and Certified Executive Coach Specialist through the Center for Coaching Certification and a member of the International Coaching Federation. Jane is the CEO and Chief Brainstormer at JaneSTORM. Her thirty-year career at Verizon and as a volunteer lead at the American Cancer Society served as her foundation for transformational coaching for life and business, workshop facilitation and public speaking.

Jane is known for bringing positive energy and curiosity to every relationship. She is an intentional listener and draws out individuals and groups with empathy, compassion, and humor. She has a proven track record in public speaking, non-profit fundraising, and event planning. Jane's high energy and bountiful ideas have contributed to her success as a program implementer and team/community interface. The JaneSTORM mission is to clear your mind clutter through thought provoking, creative and purposeful collaboration. JaneSTORM is a verb. If you need a catalyst to break through individual or team clutter, then Jane is the Storm you want in your life!

She has been happily married to Brian for 26 years and counting. He is the calm to her Storm. She has two adventurous kids, a 23-year-old daughter who lives in Nashville and a son who is a junior at SUNY New Paltz. Her family loves to travel. Creating fun adventures in other countries and throughout the United States supports clearing their mind clutter.

www.janestorm.com

LinkedIn:
https://www.linkedin.com/in/jane-mccarthy-janestorm/

Facebook: https://www.facebook.com/search/top?q=JaneStorm

Publications: *Coaching Perspectives X, Chapter 7, The Six Cs of Transformational Coaching*

Chapter 9

Loving Your Space is Loving Yourself

Janet Johnson

Over the past eighteen years, my husband and I moved four times, and two of those times were with our kids.

I have struggled with anxiety and depression for over a decade even though I'm surrounded by love. During these times, I didn't like leaving the house for fear of people seeing or judging me. I wanted to put up a front that everything was just fine.

At the same time, I didn't enjoy being in my house. We've always had too much clutter—clothes, toys, gifts, gadgets.

In 2003, we had a beautiful 2-bedroom apartment with a sunny balcony overlooking the woods. But soon, we cluttered up an entire hallway and one rented garage with wedding gifts and my husband's belongings from growing up. I put up a curtain to block the view, but it was still disturbing to me.

At that point, we stopped having people over for dinner. And rather than inviting people to our place, we met with our friends at their places or at restaurants.

I felt like a fraud when it came to our personal clutter. I felt tiny, as if I wasn't as important as our things. I carried this feeling to our new house, a beautiful 1940's style cape. It was bright and sunny, but still, we didn't host much and only met people outside of our place.

At the same time, I was working for my family's factory as the vice president. My parents both moved to the Philippines and left me in charge. With their trust, I started to feel hope for a new outlook and more energy.

In 2005, at work, I transformed myself. I had 17 employees and owed them my very best. At that point, I came out of my "Little J" persona, gathered up my courage, and started to dive in. No longer allowing it to pass me by, I grabbed life with two hands.

In my family's factory, I worked hard to streamline the space, including the shop floor. I decluttered 15 tons, yes, *that's 30,000 pounds*, of excess junk from our factory over a period of two months. I aimed to have our shop quality certified, so that meant streamlined systems and purposeful workspaces. That project for our big 20,000 square foot facility was far easier than decluttering and organizing our cape.

The reorganization worked. We became world-class quality certified, increased our prices, and gained 10 new contracts, all when I was pregnant with our first child.

Getting organized and being transparent by inviting people into my space saved our factory. Not only did it help me feel more confident and strategize more clearly, but our space also showed my customers that we had what it takes to get the job done very well.

Surprisingly, this victory didn't sustain me for the next several years. My work was too all-encompassing. By the time I pulled into our driveway at night, I felt too exhausted to work on our house. My confidence went up and down like ocean waves, never knowing how my energy or intentions would change. Although I knew how to get work done and get organized, it was the last thing I wanted to do. Our beautiful cape was a house, not a home. Living there was a blur of dog fur and too much stuff to hang onto in case we needed it one day.

When I left our factory after 17 years, eventually, I became a small business trainer. I wanted to share what I knew from my work experience with family-owned businesses that struggled with our same issues. That includes everything from money management and time management to organization. Professionally, I've helped countless small business owners increase their profitability by reorganizing their workspaces and processes.

As a trained Lean Tools expert, I know how an organized workspace increases a small business's profit in just a couple of weeks. Beyond marketing plans and branding, I had real success closing six-figure contracts. This is all due to organizing our factory, including the office and shop floor. (Recently, I wrote a workbook about my step-by-step profitability and organization techniques, and I can't wait to publish it.)

So, the big issue was that I could organize other people's spaces but not mine. My stuff was too emotional and too loaded with guilt.

Every item had a meaning. Their meaning always held more importance than I did. While my ultimate goal was always to create a home that is organized and customized for us, the stuff always shoved my plans aside.

If I let go of expensive crystal Tiffany candleholders (never been used for 15+ years, still in the box), it meant that I was wasteful.

If I donated a silver charm bracelet my husband's great aunt gave me, that meant I was ungrateful.

And, if I should ever donate the vintage green and yellow 1960's china we bought from a family friend, one who was a huge part of my life growing up, that meant that I didn't love her enough.

I had all these meanings tied up in our things that even though we hadn't used them, I felt frozen when deciding what to do with the unused/unneeded objects.

Work is much easier! I'm not emotionally attached to a box of gears, and if they're broken, I can easily scrap them. However, family stuff? Particularly family stuff from someone who passed away? That's much harder.

It wasn't just about what the meanings behind the objects were. It was also about how we displayed them. For example, we were gifted an electric frypan years ago from a family member. When that family member came to visit for dinner, you better believe that I used the same electric pan to cook our meal. It didn't matter that I preferred to use the cooking pans I used growing up with my own family. My pans had practical and sentimental value —remembering my dad's cooking, setting the table with my brother, and cleaning up afterward with my mom. It was only important to make this one person happy and use and praise her pan as if it was the holy grail.

Our former old house, the big blue colonial we moved into after the cape, was so big that we had the luxury of storing these useless items and many more. I had baby toys, my husband's baby clothes from 1978, and books that smelled too musty to read. We have a huge collection of DVDs and CDs but haven't owned a DVD or CD player since 2009.

In the blue house, we had a partially finished basement and a wall lined with shelves. It was possible to store these items, so why not? There, all these items sat for years without a second thought.

My husband and I planned to put our house on the market in March of 2020 when COVID hit. By then, we spent a good two months donating and trashing unused things. We had to put our housing goal on hold during the summer.

By August, we were back at it again.

School would start in September, and it was our goal to move to a town that was more culturally and ethnically diverse and closer to our kids' magnet schools.

My husband found the home we're in now. I fell in love with it the first time I saw it. Our new home is about 400 square feet smaller than our big 2100 square foot colonial.

If I really wanted this house, I had to change my feelings around our stuff quickly because we needed to downsize in a major way. I had to tackle the basement with a straightforward, no guts, no glory attitude. I thought of how the items I donated would be loved elsewhere. And, even after moving in, we've donated more items because there simply isn't room for all of our stuff.

After three months of realtor business back and forth, we finally moved in. On December 29th, we had a full moon. A full moon to me means new beginnings and a celebration of life. It means my ancestors are smiling down at me. I can look up at the moon and realize that my beautiful family and I are my ancestors' wildest dreams come true.

I knew this house would become our home. Beyond a house or place of residence, I'd make this home a place full of love, enriched our way, without anybody else's criticism, suggestions, or "you're supposed to do it that way!" finger-wagging objections.

I will never forget unpacking our kitchen in our new home. The former owners decorated this home in the way that I would have wanted but wouldn't be brave enough to do. I would have chosen beige walls and sensible white appliances.

Instead, they went big!

Our kitchen is a deep grape purple with cream-colored cabinets and stainless-steel appliances. The counters are black and white leathered granite that somehow feels soft and warm. The cabinets have a color-changing neon strip that lights up the floors in bright, vivid colors. The kitchen has surround sound under-cabinet speakers attached that link with the smart refrigerator—perfect for dancing. The glittery sink crystal sconce matches the modern crystal chandelier in the dining room, also purple.

With Pandora on my refrigerator, coming through the surround sound speakers, I remembered how much music lights me up. We play Tejano music when we have our Mexican food night and 1980's pop music on other nights. I play Jim Brickman when I want to relax and Whitney Houston when I want to feel amazing.

That first day, as I started packing and figuring out what I wanted, I realized that there are no rules. This is our home. To AC/DC's "It's a Long Way to the Top," loudly blasting from my fridge, the disproving commentary fell away.

Beforehand, a big obstacle that kept me from organizing my way was that I didn't want to be too "weird." I didn't want people, especially my mother-in-law, coming into my home, rolling their eyes, and wondering why I decorated my way. Then I remembered that there are thousands of Lean experts across the world—and I was one of them. Lean experts save big businesses, whole towns, and cities. I could use these same tools for my home.

At that moment, I realized, 'this is my home, and I know what I'm doing. I know how to organize, and if I don't get it right the first time, no big deal. I will just move it.'

With that, I started plotting out my cabinets using my Lean expertise. Place the most frequently used cooking utensils next to the stove. Put the dishes in the cabinet directly above the dishwasher. Put the coffee maker in the corner, away from the kids, but put the toaster—the appliance they use—in a reachable spot.'

Because our new home is significantly smaller, I wanted this house to reflect our family's needs. That means, rather than storing dusty dishware in the china hutch, I display our favorite books.

Our antique mahogany buffet now stores our board games, not antique placemats that are too fancy to use. I mean, why invent or keep placemats you can't use? Can somebody please explain that to me?

As I saw my kitchen coming together, I felt even more confident in my ability to organize and declutter well. I've carried this confidence with me throughout my home.

I talk to myself as I do this. Partially out of habit but partially because I want my kids to understand my thought process. More so, I don't want them to quit rearranging the space as they see fit. I don't want to "should" all over them. The goal is always to prioritize peace and family. Staying flexible with patience and kindness is the way to go. For example, if it wasn't for my hallway shelves, our dining table would be cluttered with mail and winter gloves.

But now that stuff has a space, we eat dinner each night together, and it's no big deal to clear the table. We set the table, light a candle, say a prayer, and talk about our day.

I would encourage you to think about your values and organize your space to support what you value the most. Think about each space having a purpose and honor that purpose. For example, our living room is our family room. It's not a storage room. Therefore, when we see boxes of stuff cluttering up our space (even when it's meant to go out in 2 weeks), we move it. We don't let it sit there. If it doesn't honor the space, we move it.

I'd also recommend not running out and buying the latest

organizational tools because they're on sale or match your color scheme. Think about how your mind works. For example, don't buy horizontal filing trays if you're more of a visual/tiered thinker.

When shopping online, I put the items I need right now into my wishlist and check on it a couple of days later. I'm at a 50/50. I realize that some items I really needed and others were just shiny-object distractions.

Also, you don't need to fill up every space like a Jenga tower. It's OK to open up a cabinet and see that it's half full or near empty. I've known plenty of people who feel insecure about not having enough or not storing enough.

If something causes you guilt or reminds you of a negative experience, don't put it out and consider decluttering it. On the flip side, if something makes you smile when you see it, display it. I have a rainbow film on many of our windows. I put it there not only for privacy but because I love how the light streams in and makes our home more festive.

I also like to display my mom's quilts. My mom worked really hard on these quilts for us, so why keep them in a cabinet when they can be on display, and I can see them every day?

When it comes to moms (and other elders who mean well), forget the mothering shoulds. It's a different time, and our families have different needs from way back when. Kindly thank them for their advice and just do it your way.

I'm now in my 40s and am so grateful. This is the best time of my life! All of the guilt, the "shoulds," and other people's criticism just fall off me.

To me, this is what embracing your space means. It's turning a house into your home. Each room should serve its purpose, outside of storing random stuff. Each room should have something that catches your eye and makes you smile.

Do you consider your house a home? If not, please know that loving your space is akin to loving yourself. There are no rules! Start with one corner and one smile. And, perhaps some AC/DC on Pandora.

About Janet Johnson

Janet Johnson, the Profit Breakthrough Coach, is the CEO and Founder of Quail Run Ventures, LLC.

She teaches her clients how to cultivate order, peace, and prosperity so they can create freedom for themselves and the ones they love.

Janet has the greatest compassion for family-owned businesses and acknowledges her clients as brilliant and capable.

Relying upon her 26 years of experience, she teaches entrepreneurs how to see the value they bring and how they stand in the power of creating life-changing solutions.

Using her Sacred Money Archetypes® Certification, Janet helps her clients overcome challenges by embracing their strengths and inherent gifts. For entrepreneurs, she helps them empower their pricing and sales conversation to grow their business and help as many families as possible.

Janet earned her Bachelor's Degree in Management and Master's Degree in Business Administration from Quinnipiac University.

www.MyMoneyPivot.com

Chapter 10

Layers of Life

Sheri Giancarlo

As I pulled into the driveway, my mind began taking notes. Nothing special about this house—a ranch, not neglected but it needed some TLC. The worn path in the gravel driveway leading to the house indicated the side door would be my entry point. As I got closer to the house, the neglect began to emerge like a Monet painting; far away the landscape is crystal clear, up close the individual brush strokes are apparent. I did not dare hang onto the railing as it tilted away from its base where rot had its way. As I knocked on the door and waited, I could see through the disheveled curtain barely attached on the other side of the door. My eyes met with the messy assortment of stuff that littered the space that I was about to enter.

"Space, the final frontier," a familiar phrase spoken during Star Trek's introduction, implied a boundless place. I am feeling "spaced out" implies a foggy state of mind. "Get out of my space" suggests an area with definite boundaries. No matter how space is referenced, it all means the same thing: it is a place, a somewhere, somewhere to go, somewhere to stay, somewhere to leave. It is a something, something to possess, something to desire. It can be tangible or intangible, but one thing is certain. As humans, we occupy it. There are all kinds of spaces: home space, workspace, play space, safe space, outer space, my space, your space. For humans, a home provides space to keep our belongings, and its size often correlates with the amount of stuff one possesses. Comedian George Carlin defined a house as "a pile of stuff with a cover on it."

After several knocks on the door, my client finally answered and we cordially greeted each other. I thought to myself that if the sun porch was any indication of what the rest of the house looks like, I understand why it took her so long to get to the door. Through the door, I was surprised that I was not overcome by the disgusting scent of a litter box, rotting food, cigarette smoke, or the putrid smell of dead rodents. Although I had little hope for this project, I took notes and shared polite comments. I have been in many homes, but this one was overwhelming! I could feel the pulse of suppression, smell the air of desperation, and see the wreckage of one's soul.

She was a kind, older lady, small in stature. She appeared tired, but eager to talk to me about her plans. She was able to carve out two seats at the kitchen table so we could discuss me designing a new kitchen for her. Everything showed its age. It was dingy, dented, worn out and outdated. She was the house, the house was her, and I understood her desire for change. Sadly, I told her that a new kitchen at this time was not a good idea. I explained that I could not even move around in the space to obtain the dimensions. She began to cry and succumbed to her reality with posture and words spelling defeat. The problem could not be solved with a new kitchen, it was deeper.

The layers of life were piled thick in this home, like blankets on a bed in the midst of winter, only there was little comfort or warmth. She was drowning in left-behind belongings of her adult children and countless books that lined bookshelves. Belongings acquired from dead relatives were shoved into corners while her office served double duty as a supposed sanctuary for her hobbies. Her home was evidence of the turmoil in her brain. It was the physical manifestation of unfinished business. There was no more room; none in the home, none in her brain. Yet for some reason, the two of us were put together that day to acknowledge she had nowhere to go.

In the kitchen, my eye was drawn to three large coffee cans sitting on top of a rolling cart tucked tightly next to the kitchen sink. They were filled with pens, pencils, and markers. She expended thought and effort implementing this storage plan for enough writing supplies to sustain an elementary school for a year, but explained that she "keeps them for her grandchildren."

I could tell she felt ashamed and embarrassed about the state of her home but at the same time relieved in sharing her secret with me. She felt at ease with me as she continued to tell me the stories of her life, about her inattentive husband, entitled children and her most recent tragedy, an injured arm from a car accident that further interfered with any organization. From our conversation, she understood that a new kitchen would represent a band-aid on an infected wound.

That day, my role had shifted from a professional in design to the needed company of a compassionate stranger. I gave her hope, and that is what she paid me for. I do not know if she ever completed the tasks that we outlined, but that day at her kitchen table she understood she needed to embrace her space in order to have a better one.

Many of us have been where my client was in some form or another. Thirteen years ago, my sister and I had to clear out my parents' home after their deaths. My sister moved swiftly through everything, while I considered each item slowly. I am thankful she was there as the process of emptying a home where I had once lived was overwhelming and very emotional. The attic held the dolls I once loved, the Barbies I played with for hours, beloved high school art projects. Items my mother cherished and kept either for herself or for us, baby books, christening gowns, her wedding dress, we, her daughters, now handled and acknowledged each piece with tenderness. The dumpster parked in the driveway like a baby bird with its mouth wide open ready to swallow up the leftovers from our lives as trash whose purpose served. It was surreal.

In the cellar, an obstacle course of empty boxes piled from floor to ceiling was the first challenge. In my heart, I knew the boxes were evidence of my mother's catalog shopping habit—

something she did to fill the void left by my father's passing and a multitude of other losses.

My mother's space, once filled with the bustling life of two daughters, a husband, pets, and frequent visits from family and friends, was reduced to a pile of boxes. She longed for the past, and now I did too.

Urgency made "discard" the name of the game my sister and I played that day; it was not a fun game! We found more boxes filled with important contents from my late maternal grandparents, evidence my mother was faced with the same task my sister and I were now experiencing. We paused to read some letters we found from those boxes, written in the handwriting we were so familiar with. We discovered a side to our mother that we were not privy to growing up. She wrote loving words to her parents from a thousand miles away telling them how she liked her new life that rested on an impromptu decision to ride off on the back of some guy's motorcycle.

How does one discard someone's life? The collection left behind is a representation of their existence, tangible items to hold, to see, and smell as we cling to their memory. I was faced with the immediate task of retrieving my mother's belongings at the insistence of the nursing home. The bed, still warm, was needed for the next patient.

It took five years before I could open the last box of my mother's belongings. This was the final goodbye, the things that made my mother recognizable: her black and burgundy square rimmed glasses, her false teeth foretelling of her smile. We come into this world with nothing and leave with nothing. What happens in between is living, living in space, surrounded by stuff that in the end loses its identity when it meets the fate of a dumpster.

I have come to understand the burden of "stuff" as I get older. I see the layers of my life adding up. Unemployment during the pandemic gave me the opportunity to purge "stuff." One day, I managed the heart wrenching chore of emptying bins labeled with grades of my grown son's earliest education. Every mother's prized possession, the macaroni necklace, the paper with his first scribbles on it that would soon evolve into his name, three letters, I-A-N...Somewhere along the way, Ian became interested in the environment, and now lives a life dedicated to serving the environment. He shops at Goodwill, has a vegan lifestyle, a used vehicle, and promotes environmental causes in his daily work. He values his space differently than I do. He does not want to have a lot of possessions; he wants to live a life free from the burden of "stuff." He has enlightened and inspired me, and I find myself thinking about my stuff, why I have it, what will happen to it when I am gone.

Now, the little boy who once released butterflies in the garden and caught a fish with his Scooby-Doo fishing pole makes me question how to embrace space. If the possessions we acquire are essential to our identity, do they define us? As the layers of my life stack up, everyday I ponder their thickness and wonder how to embrace my future space.

About Sheri Giancarlo

Sheri was born creative and has always been involved with art in some form or another, but it was interior spaces that fascinated her the most. As a young girl when other children would be playing together outside, Sheri was drawing floor plans not even knowing what a designer or an architect was. How humans interact with space, space she can imagine in 3-D in her mind from a piece of paper, would eventually become a cornerstone of her career. Her innate knack for design benefitted family and friends throughout the years. In 2010, Sheri graduated with Honors from The Art Institute of Pittsburgh with a Bachelor of Science Degree in Interior Design. This allowed her to turn her natural talent into a professional reality.

Sheri is the owner of Withinteriors and believes "within your home resides your story." Utilizing an effective and efficient business model, Sheri works closely with her clients and reveals custom designs reflecting who they are from within. Sheri loves the thrill of pleasing her clients with design concepts they never thought possible. Sheri resides in Lebanon, Connecticut with her husband of 29 years, Phill, and her dogs, Abbott and Mia. Their son Ian recently moved to Denver, Colorado to pursue his career in environmental causes and to be closer to the mountains rendering them true empty nesters. Sheri enjoys spending time at home in her backyard (described as a "haven" by many), driving her convertible, spending time with friends, gardening and visiting botanical gardens, and shopping, especially for her clients.

www.withinteriors.com

Release

Lianne Dixon

"Here's what I know about clearing. You can't ignore it forever if you want to live a life that's complete."

Christina Fitch, DO, MPH

"This was a true clearing out so the new has space to enter. And it feels so good. I wish I had done it sooner, yet I recognize that the timing was divine."

Audra Garling Mika, MA

"Embracing space is embracing ourselves and making time for others and what matters most in life. Choose you. Choose family. Choose love. Don't choose your material "stuff." Your final moments will come, so make the most of each one – now."

Chapter 11

What Else Needs to Go?

Lianne Dixon

Clearing, decluttering, and organizing are old friends of mine.

Having moved 17 times from the time I was born until I was married at the age of 30, then an additional four times over the course of my 13-year marriage, I am happy to report experiencing little emotional attachment to things. In fact, I rarely think twice about running through a closet with the intention of dropping off a carload of stuff to Goodwill. Experience, however, has taught me that not all moves are equal. Some are "easy," and others pull on every ounce of strength you can muster to release what you love, including those you love, and to stretch onto a new path.

One of the most challenging moves in my life to date was moving from my prairie hometown of Winnipeg, Manitoba, Canada, to be with my now ex-husband. He was in the United States Air Force at the time, and that move had me release belongings, my home, my career, my parents, my family, my friends, and my country. None of it was easy, but I had met this man who loved me better than anyone else up until then (including myself), and the dream of love and building a home and family pulled me forward and beyond where I was.

Knowing this, you might appreciate how it didn't occur to me —not even once—that I would have issues releasing anything following my divorce. We had, after all, been separated for five years and divorced for about a year and a half before the move. Choosing to co-parent and share a home throughout that time, I was confident that I had effectively dealt with everything in my counselor's office. I believed that while I might experience a twinge or two of grief along the way, it would be a completely liberating process.

Well, it turns out, the whole thing was more of a challenge than I imagined. I was surprised to find that divorce, preparing my home to sell, moving, and downsizing all carried an emotional toll and struggle even after years of counseling, an impressive list of moves, and self-professed detachment to things. Having these experiences rolled into one that demanded I release and open doors to the inner places of my heart and psyche that I had conveniently compartmentalized and safely tucked away.

For example, while preparing the house to sell, I was cleaning and organizing the basement kitchen and family room. I had built this space in the basement to launch a cake business. The business didn't work out as planned and I let clutter accumulate in the space. It became one of the few places in the house that I ignored. I didn't consciously acknowledge why junk accumulated there or why I never took the time to clean it, but I knew I ignored it—a lot.

"Why? Why had I ignored this space for so long?" I angrily swore at myself while working through the piles of clutter to prepare the home to sell. It had, after all, been 11 years since we had the basement finished and the kitchen built for the cake business.

Eleven years!

I swore at myself again for having feelings, and then a rush of memories came flooding back, overriding my anger and self-reprimanding. The truth was the cake business hadn't been the only dream I had for that space. I had envisioned pizza nights, board games, and a basement full of my son's friends to entertain on weekends. I was ready for every teenage craving, Friday night gathering, and birthday party, armed with an industrial size convection oven that could bake 200 cookies at a time. This space was going to be the ultimate family room and teenage retreat.

And that's when I started to sob.

Scrubbing the inside of the oven, I began to remember what my heart could never forget.

This space had become a physical representation of lost dreams. It held the painful memory of the first night I realized my marriage was on the brink of destruction, only days before I launched the cake business. Then, years later, when the marriage was entirely in the toilet, it became my ex's living space through the first couple years of our separation. By the time he found his way to the guest bedroom, all my dreams of what "could have been" had died completely or were well into the grieving process. I had no desire to return to a space that I had created with so much hope and joy.

Texting some of my dearest friends in the midst of the tsunami of emotions that I experienced that evening, feeling angry and irritated at my feelings, they encouraged me just to let it all go. So that's what I did. I leaned into the moment and allowed all the anger and sorrow trapped inside to flow through me. I "ugly" cried and scrubbed for about a half-hour, then everything shifted.

Suddenly, leaving it all behind, I found myself praying for the family who would purchase the home. The tidal wave of anger and grief had come crashing. It consumed me. Then it was complete. I had done a lot of emotional clearing and decluttering through grief work and counseling over the last several years, and I'm convinced that all that remained was one last good cry. One final goodbye because all that remained afterward was calmness.

I had prayed for the home's next family long before that night. I prayed while painting the walls and kitchen cabinets, reminiscing about the love and laughter that had also very much been a part of the house's history. I blessed the space as I worked for all the new beginnings ahead.

But on this night, in addition to the happiness I wished for, I visualized them enjoying the family room and kitchen in a way we never could. Clearing the clutter, facing what remained of my anger and sadness, finally meant a complete release. Other parts of the house needed clearing, but none of those areas "hooked" me. Stuff is stuff, and it's okay to let it go. From that point on, I found myself moving through the process with a great degree of ease and joyful anticipation for what lay ahead.

Here's what I know about clearing. You can't ignore it forever if you want to live a life that's complete. This type of work is silently demanding. *It will not go away until you choose to do it.* Take whatever time you need, it's your process after all. When it's all said and done, you'll know that putting it off kept you emotionally and creatively constipated in ways you didn't expect. You'll also realize you possessed more strength than you imagined up until now.

So what happened next?

My adventure took me down the path of downsizing. And true to form, I magically believed that too would be a piece of cake. Honestly, I had decided only to take a few of the larger home items, my immediate personal belongings, some of my son's things, and a few gadgets from the kitchen. I was leaving everything else behind, so how hard could a move like that be?

Well, just because you're not taking it with you doesn't mean you don't have to deal with it. But at that point, it *was* just stuff. Overall, the work was physically demanding and required more time than I had anticipated.

Moving into my new space is when things got interesting again. Just when I thought I was done and couldn't possibly throw out, recycle, or give away one more thing—BOOM! It's time for another *"come to Jesus"* moment. The new place was even smaller than I thought, requiring me to release even more. Faced with the decision of paying for storage or just trusting that I would have everything I needed when I needed it, I found myself asking once again, "What do I really love? What do I really need? And what else can I release?"

Those have become the BIG questions in my life. They are the very questions that give voice to Spirit and guidance. As I continue to grow and deepen my spiritual experience, I have come to appreciate that Spirit wants to provide us with everything we want. In response to my prayer or intention, I imagine Spirit saying, "Yes! Yes! I'd love to! Now tell me, what are you prepared to release in order to allow for that to happen?"

So there I was, in my smaller than expected apartment, hands in the air, calling out, "Are you kidding me!? What else could I possibly give away!?" And that's when it hit me. It was never about the "stuff" or the "downsizing." Nevertheless, more "stuff" needed to go, and downsizing needed to happen because on a practical level, there just wasn't any space. On the spiritual plane, these actions forged the path to my next spiritual challenge.

This place, the precipice of a new spiritual challenge, is the place where I found myself (once again) naked before God.

No longer hiding behind any "thing," I curiously explored the possibility of what release means outside the material framework I had been working within. New questions emerged. No longer distracted by my "stuff," I peered more deeply into the many layers and aspects of myself. This, of course, was not the first time I had asked that question or taken a meaningful dive into this type of release. I had done this work before, but this most recent journey was on a path not yet traveled and perspective not yet experienced. I could feel the lessons and new knowing penetrating at a different level and taking root. Or maybe I finally arrived at a place where I was determined to pay attention.

This space of realization enables me to look at clearing and releasing daily, asking Spirit questions like: "Who am I without fear?" and "Who am I without struggle?" or "Show me, Spirit, who I am without all that extra baggage." New questions emerge, and I find myself shifting in subtle and not so subtle ways. I'm less reactive. I'm more resilient. Ready to experience life from a different perspective in order to arrive at a more authentic version of who I am, I'm now willing to "drop everything" because honestly, I believe that's Spirit's way of dancing us through this crazy, wonderful life.

At least that's where the road has led me so far, but this adventure is only just beginning, and new discoveries await.

"Spirit, show me what I need to release to make way for my authentic self to emerge and for the benefit of peace and joy to lead me through life's many paths."

About Lianne Dixon

Lianne Dixon is a certified family coach with a Bachelor's in Social Work. Her mission is to guide and support parents who are tired of the clash, conflict, and disrespectful attitudes that frequently accompany adolescence. Releasing patterns that no longer serve their families, she introduces parents to high-impact strategies that immediately begin to build respect, trust, and strengthen communication between them and their teen, to finally end the struggle and create a more peaceful home.

www.gettingrealcoach.com

Chapter 12

A Shrine of a Room

Christina Fitch, DO, MPH

Every item in the room, from the color of the paint on the walls to the bedspread, was lovingly and collaboratively chosen. The whole intent of allowing the boys at the age of eight to make their own decisions about this room in my home was so they would want to spend as much time in it as possible.

I had bought this house three and a half years prior in an effort to move closer to family and to have a space that everyone could use for daily enjoyment and for holidays. As a single woman, buying a home in a suburb with three bedrooms and two and a half baths seems excessive. But my vision was of 20 people feasting around a Thanksgiving table, 10 people scattered around the Christmas tree surrounded by wrapping paper and gifts, and five people sledding down the side hill on freshly fallen snow. My nephews were part of every group I imagined.

My nephews, twins, much anticipated and desired, had shockingly caused a large rift in the family since their birth. Due to their parents' divorce when they were infants and parenting decisions subsequent to that based on anger and revenge, our family strife had increased to the point where lines of communication were very weakened. After the purchase of the house and the decorating of this room with two twin captain beds, an end table between them, and a bureau in the corner, those weak lines broke.

I kept that room exactly as it had been decorated for the boys for all those years because somewhere deep down I felt that if the opportunity ever arose for them to come back to visit, that it would have meaning to them to see that nothing had changed. The signs with their names above the beds from the Boston Childrens' museum would still be there as would the afghans I had crocheted in their favorite colors. In the closet would be the uno cards we liked to play, the kazoo they made a racket with, and my old stuffed toys to keep them company if they ever spent the night. Over the years, I mailed them little bits and pieces—the remaining pokemon stickers that didn't fit on the wall, the camo tent kit that they enjoyed hanging between the windows—to remind them of the joy we had in creating this room. I never heard from them and my heart broke into little pieces. Or maybe I should say that I ate my heart out. The grief and loss of what was planned for and lost literally made me sick.

After many years of working in the hospital, the opportunity came for me to work from home. I was anxious about the huge shift in my career path and how emotionally trying it would be to spend my days alone. But it turns out that the whole world seemed to start working from home at the same time due to the pandemic. So, we all felt isolated and had to learn the art of Zoom. I loved being at home, cultivating each room to serve me. I got a standing desk on wheels and moved wherever the sun was. But then I realized that I spent my entire workday in the den or living room which is where I wanted to relax at night. The computer was always in my line of sight after hours.

I started trying to envision my ideal workspace and realized unless I was going to invest a lot of money in making a new space (refinishing the basement, for example) in an already cavernous house for one, I would have to repurpose old space.

My mind rebelled at changing anything in their room (the boys' room as I called it), and yet I could see the wastefulness. I had only had three nights with other children staying overnight in that room. To tell the truth, it hurt to have other children using their things. Daily, I would pass by their room every time I walked from the bedroom down the stairs, and I felt the oppressiveness of the empty dark room, curtains shut to keep out dust and prevent fading. My spirit knew that it was time and yet my mind, my strongest tool and my biggest enemy, fought against change. If I got rid of their beds, would that mean that I was giving up hope that they would ever stay here? If I used the room for myself, did that mean that I had lost the original mission of the house, which was to unify my broken family? It took three months of discussions with my long-standing therapist and my dear life coach to reframe the transition of my beloved nephews' room into my home office as a positive and necessary step forward. Finally, a short and turbulent romantic relationship gave me the kickstart I needed to make the change.

As so often happens, when I opened the door to that possibility, all the pieces rapidly slipped into place. I started by reaching out to a friend to see if she knew anyone who could use the beds. Within a day I had a plan set up for a family in need to come pick them up, which they did just a few days later. The next day, the housecleaner was available to give it a deep clean. Two days later, my neighbor helped me move my home desk and my work standing desk into the room. I was considering painting the teal room my favorite color, purple, but found that the color was so soothing, I didn't want to change it. I kept the curtains and the lamps, but brought additional items from other rooms to make this room as comfortable and peaceful as possible. The finishing grace was finding a six-pot planter that I loved which allowed me to expand my plant collection into yet another room. Over the next two months, I tweaked the location of things to make everything work well for me, to support the life I wanted. Having everything in its place was the encouragement I needed to go through the piles of paperwork that had accumulated around the house. I spent a couple months shredding, recycling, and filing in a space that made me feel inspired and supported.

Now I can share about it, with only a few tears in the writing. When I start my workday, I am excited to be here. It has a north and east facing window, which meets my sun standards. It has plants to purify the air. There is a standing desk and a kneeling chair to keep my posture healthy. The laptops, printer, cellphones, shredder, and charger station all work. I know where all my work and home files are. I can find what I need when I need it.

I have not missed having a room that I do not use and that contributes to my sorrow just by its existence. I sent the remaining personal items to my nephews as Christmas gifts and all the linens went with the beds. This was a true clearing out so the new has space to enter. And it feels so good. It was not an easy process. I wish I had done it sooner, yet I recognize that the timing was divine. The steps were necessary and could not be rushed. It is in reflection that I have processed the journey to a point of clarity, which contributes to my feeling of being cared for by the universe. That is what I wish for you. Whatever you are facing, whatever emotions are tied to making a change in your space, please know that on the other side of the struggle is ease. I can see now that the shrine of a room served no purpose and was holding me back from blessings.

About Christina Fitch, DO, MPH

Christina "Ina" Fitch is a world traveler, having visited or worked in 35 countries, living out of one suitcase for months at a time. As a hospice and palliative care physician, she has cared for people around the world. She loves to teach clinically as well as didactically, sharing her love of global health, health ethics, serious illness conversations, and opioid management to learners from all backgrounds.

Owning a suburban colonial home, with more space than most extended families in most countries could claim, has spurred a flair for both interior and garden design. And most importantly, it has offered a venue for hosting and entertaining chosen family.

Chapter 13

The Art of Closing a Life

Audra Garling Mika

"I go to seek a Great Perhaps," are French poet Francois Rabelais' last words.

Referring to the afterlife and something he hoped was real, Rabelais inspires Miles Halter, the main character in John Green's wildly popular young adult novel, *Looking for Alaska*, to go seek his own "Great Perhaps." Miles is obsessed with famous people's final words, not death, and he now wishes to find bold, beautiful adventures and transcend life's everyday minutia. Miles wants to take action and to live his life on purpose.

In January of that year, my sister, Debra, called to tell me that our mother had collapsed and was being rushed, unconscious, to the hospital by ambulance. For the next eight weeks, my father, Debra, my other sister, Laura, and I fought to save Mom. Days after she was admitted to the hospital with sepsis, we said our goodbyes on Super Bowl Sunday only to learn that on Monday an amputation would save her life. With her right foot cut off, she rebounded for the month of March. By the time April approached, her body and soul had finally surrendered. She was now ready to seek her own Great Perhaps.

My mother's illness gave me a glimpse of her playful side despite her deteriorating condition. Her death crystalized my view on life. Days before she died, she told her nurses and physical therapists that she appreciated them so much that she had redrafted her will to name *them* her beneficiaries. She also told the doctors all about her funny and valiant friend, Vicki, who won her battle against breast cancer but lost her breasts. Mom said the two of them would "start a group called 'The footless, the boobless, and the toothless;' we just need to find toothless."

"Thank you," were the last words I spoke to my mom on April 2, 2017.

Saying goodbye to my mother—and soon after cleaning out our family homestead with my sisters—taught me radical acceptance. Not merely tolerance but a full-on embracing of reality. I came to understand that a complete and total acceptance of life exactly as it is right now is necessary to move forward.

An abundant life begins when you appreciate what you already have. I think all of us are at our best when things are at their worst. For me, a personal crisis clarifies my priorities. Maybe that's why so often death teaches us how to live. A bigger life begins when you know – really know – what you want...and you make the choice to go get it regardless of circumstances.

My bigger life began when my mother died.

I finalized my divorce exactly two years after my mom died. Following 14 years in a mismatched marriage, it was time to live my life authentically and model for my boys what self-respect, confidence, and joy look like. Across town, I found a small ranch a third the size of the Colonial that my former husband and I shared. Slowly and methodically, I once again started the project of dismantling a family home. By June of 2019, with the help of professional movers and the emotional and organizational support of my sisters and their partners, I moved into my new home. Living in what I call "the dollhouse" with one bath, nearly no kitchen cabinet space, a washer and dryer stacked on top of each other in the corner of the kitchen where my dream pantry should be, I embrace my new space. It's filled with homey, positive energy.

When I moved out after my divorce, I hadn't fully recovered physically, emotionally, or mentally from sorting, decluttering, consigning, emptying, and selling my parents' home two years earlier. We had lived there for 35 years. But, life—especially a bigger, more authentic one—must go on, right?

My mother's death brought me back to life. The secret to a life well-lived lies in actually living it. Making choices and priorities daily that align with our values, desires, and dreams. Living means not waiting for that false concept called "readiness" or when we feel no fear. Neither a state of readiness nor fearlessness exists. We must take action and move forward with our fears and doubts safely stowed in the backseat. We must never let fear take the wheel. If we do, we let our doubts and small thinking cut short our life's journey.

When I met my sisters in the hospital to see my mother lying unconscious in January 2017, I stroked her hair. "You're okay," I told her. "You are okay, sweet girl." Almost overnight, the daughters became the parents.

Three months later, with our mother's fight for her life, her death, and memorial service behind us, the sisters got to work.

My father made it abundantly clear that he was done. He was done managing a large Victorian home in the heart of Goshen and keeping it *Architectural Digest* worthy. No more to-do lists, no more projects. Dad wanted to live out the remainder of his life as a cheerful, lighthearted widower. And, that is exactly what he did.

My sisters and I honored our mother by respecting our father's wish to sell the large Victorian in which we grew up and where we hosted countless important family events. Now an aging widower, my dad simply could not keep up with the work an old home requires or the politics of a shared driveway or our home's large lawn and lush gardens.

My sisters and I likely postponed our grief and avoided an obsession over legal, financial, and logistical issues related to death by getting busy prepping the house for sale. Traveling from out of town to meet in Goshen, we learned to embrace each other's pace in pouring through the thousands of collections our mother kept: years' worth of school artwork and report cards; every single letter and holiday card; Wedgewood kitchen pottery and dishware; glasses; Byers Choice carolers; and items like scarves, handbags, shoes, and coats. The sorting into toss, gift, and donate piles continued with each of us taking a carload full everytime we visited. When all three of us couldn't coordinate to be together, we left individual piles for the others. We could not get the house emptied fast enough.

I wanted my childhood home sold so Dad could rest, relax, and retreat. Laura, Deb, Dad, and I spent every weekend between May and August 2017 cleaning, organizing, sorting, and emptying our family home of 35 years.

My sisters and I were rarely in town at the same time to get the work done. Sometimes we were. Mostly we weren't. And we certainly experienced different emotions – or at least the pace of them – in saying goodbye to our mom and our home in the same short period. After all, I spent most of my high school years in this house. Deb was beginning college the summer we moved in, and Laura came back briefly after graduating college and before marrying and moving out.

We divided to conquer. We started in our parents' bedroom, then bounced to the kitchen. Sorting, sifting, tossing as we went. Debra and Laura handled emptying the dining room hutch and buffet and Dad's home office. I joke that I grew up in a museum because my mom collected and decorated with antique furniture found at auction, and we were rarely allowed to sit in the living room. Each unique piece came with drawers, lots of drawers. The highboy chest in the foyer took Laura and me *hours* to empty.

Why did we feel compelled to go through every piece of paper? Probably because we get that so many who grieve wish they had had the chance to go through their loved one's belongings after they died. We knew we were in an enviable position in so many ways.

We hired an expert to run the estate sale in early August. With my organizational skills, Laura's decorating talent, and Deb's selling savvy, we easily could've run the estate sale ourselves and saved thousands in the process. Unfortunately, logistics like timing and geography got in the way. We had a father to relocate and a house to sell. And, yes, we also outsourced the selling of the house. Again, we weren't on site to handle all the myriad details; my sisters had demanding jobs and I had young children who needed me.

It's a funny thing. When a parent dies all the grief you feel, which is love with nowhere to go, gets poured into the other parent. We lavished love, attention, and so much joy onto our father. We felt honored to help him find his final home: a large apartment in his favorite town and near his friends and many volunteer organizations. In some ways, my sisters and I believe it took us losing our mother to find our father. With the stressors of an overly critical and ever present spouse removed, our dad's health issues subsided. Certainly, being rid of the burden of the housekeeping expense and workload, our father seemed to grow younger! He ventured out with friends most nights and began to exude a playfulness we rarely saw. Although he always loved us and was 100% invested in our family, our mother often overshadowed him. Once free from this dynamic, he embraced his new freedom to express himself more. His last three Christmas and birthday cards to us contained sentimental expressions and an outpouring of emotion. Regular Friday night happy hours and Sunday afternoons filled with football games and soup making, as well as road trips and an excursion abroad, were among his favorite adventures at the end. With levity and laughter, he flourished in his final three years before joining my mother. He always made our return visit home to Goshen a special event.

No matter how far apart we traveled or how busy our lives became, my sisters and I always embraced the sacred space of visiting with our parents and routinely returning to Goshen's Murray Avenue, our Garling homebase.

Like my mother, who dreaded wakes and funerals, I am no

fan of the macabre. Yet, when we embrace life's bigger picture, we see the role death plays in focusing a life. We all know we *should* live every day like it's our last because someday it will be, but how many of us *actually do* live this way? Perhaps strategic living lies in embracing each day's many present moments while also keeping an eye on how our daily actions impact our future and, ultimately, our legacy. Live authentically day to day, month to month, year to year, and decade to decade. Then, watch it add up to a legacy worth bestowing.

The art of closing a life – especially our parents' – includes more than sad goodbyes. It involves physical, mental, and emotional strain. Not only did we lose our parents, we also lost our family home. And, now we were the ones in charge.

On Christmas 2020, the Garling Five shrunk to the Garling three. Unlike so many other families who lose connection after a death, the Garling Girls remain tight and together, continuing family traditions and planting seeds that will grow new favorite traditions, too.

We all know the only constant in life is change, and I've learned to embrace current conditions and circumstances because they are temporary. I know that all experiences can bring joy and meaning; even my parents' passing and the end of our family home.

For most of us, decluttering our physical spaces is trendy – a concept and lucrative industry that occupies much of our time and attention. Tips and tricks of reorganizing and decluttering abound in magazines, books, TV shows, and design philosophies to show us the way to better mental health.

What about decluttering our mental space? What about embracing our personal pace in handling and radically accepting the hardest change of all: grief and loss?

The attention we give to thoughts that either don't matter or matter too much often creates such unnecessary mental strain when we don't handle them swiftly. Yet, we can't move to action until we first accept and embrace our personal pace.

Culling through the countless possessions that belonged to someone we lost, can transport us back to a meaningful time and place spent with the people we hold most dear. So, while I was tempted to, I never said, "I wish I could light a match," about the overwhelming work of emptying our home. I knew better. Many do not get the gift my sisters and I got in experiencing the endearing reunion with our favorite memories which heals and moves us forward – if we let it. The memory lane trip is a fun one, but loved ones' possessions are not them. Things can't bring people back. Not even their most cherished possessions.

I know the items my mother and father each loved the most (ever the planner, my mother even wrote a list of them in her journal!), and they left even these treasures behind – reminding me that we really can't take anything with us. As Billy Graham said, "I never saw a U-haul behind a hearse."

In my early years of teaching, I studied Wiggins and McTighe's Understanding by Design, which is a framework for lesson planning that requires course designers to start with the end in mind and work backwards from there. These principles are often called Backward Design, and they shed light on how we should live our lives. After all, we all know how our life ends: we will die. We need to think of how we might lessen the burden on family members left behind, and plan accordingly – now.

What can you donate, toss, or give away today? Choose to not stay stuck under your stuff. Embracing space is embracing ourselves and making time for others and what matters most in life. Choose you. Choose family. Choose love. Don't choose your material "stuff." Your final moments will come, so make the most of each one – now.

We must free ourselves on all counts to continue moving forward. We must embrace our space and our pace. I work to fully embrace my mental, emotional, and physical spaces. It's the lesson that keeps coming up. It's not a one and done; it's a process that demands time and respect. It's work worth doing because I want to be present for and enjoy the journey. I will work to stay open to people, my surroundings, and an abundance of opportunities awaiting me.

"Goshen is just a memory now," Laura said in late January 2021. We had just cleaned and cleared our dad's apartment. The chapter of Goshen, New York, was over. I totally disagreed, and still do, but embraced her interpretation as just that – hers. No matter where I am, I will never feel like I can't or don't need to go home to Goshen – literally or figuratively.

As of June 2021, my parents are together again, their ashes buried in our Garling family plot at the stunningly beautiful Kensico Cemetery in Valhalla, New York. I will visit my parents there, and I will still drive down Goshen's Murray Avenue to visit our Victorian. And, when I can't get back to Goshen or Kensico, my parents left such a strong sense of home and family in me – and in each of my sisters – that I can embrace their presence in my dreams and memories.

While writing this chapter, I have wondered, *What do you do when you have found your home and you can't stay there?*

The answers come in the asking. I realized I call home more than Goshen and our Victorian house. Geographic homes also steal my heart: Boston, England, Washington, DC, and now my sweet ranch house on the hill in Connecticut where I live with my two young boys in a home filled with laughter and love.

My heart resides in multiple places simultaneously.

In January 2020, nearly four years after my mom passed, almost a year after my divorce, a year before my father passed, and just in time for the dormant season of COVID-19, I began to more earnestly seek my Great Perhaps. For starters, I knew I wasn't destined to stay a classroom teacher, and I knew I needed a high-vibe tribe. For me, a home includes surrounding myself with all the right people to catapult me forward emotionally, spiritually, and professionally. Never underestimate the power of people to anchor you, bring you home, and inspire you to live and love more deeply.

May our journeys home to our most authentic selves be the gift we each choose to give ourselves – sooner rather than later.

About Audra Garling Mika

As a writing coach, Audra Garling Mika serves young people by helping them launch lives they love. Inspiring and empowering students in both the college process and career development are two signature services she offers at The Write Fit Career & College Prep Coaching.

Audra has worked with thousands of high school and college students on the college and career search process, helping them land top-choice college acceptances and fulfilling jobs. She has also polished numerous clients' business and personal writing projects and edited best-selling books on Amazon.

She also supports writers of all ages who are ready to tell their stories in a public way as their story editor, website editor, and proofreader.

As a former high school English teacher, university career services director, and communications professional, Audra directs her clients on customized paths to find their professional and personal right fit, encouraging all of them to dream big.

www.thewritefitprep.com

Receive

Mara Dowler

"With awareness, intention, patience, and commitment, you can transform your outer world and your inner world from chaos to calm."

Elizabeth B. Hill, MSW

"By releasing the stress and weight of objects and burdens, my mind is free to be openly creative, to focus on my work, enjoy time with family, and be open to receive."

Donna Finocchiaro

"I had found my passion, my driving force in life, and the bonus was that I was helping others to change their lives for the better, too."

Chapter 14

From Chaos to Calm

Mara Dowler

Imagine yourself treading water in the middle of the deep end of a crowded swimming pool. It's a hazy, hot, humid summer day. The surface of the water is cluttered with various pool toys, brightly colored noodles, and all shapes and sizes of floats and rafts. The volume of noise around you seems to amplify; and your arms and legs suddenly feel as if they have weights attached to them from trying to stay afloat. Then you hear the shrill *phweeeeeet!* of the lifeguard's whistle, and he announces, "Adult Swim!"

Children groan but dutifully scamper out of the pool, as it gradually empties around you. The pool accessories and toys are gathered up, one by one. Someone nudges an inflatable raft in your direction with kindness in her eyes and a gentle smile on her face. The heavy haze softly lifts revealing a beautiful, deep blue, cloudless sky as the sunlight dances on the water giving it a brilliant sparkly effect.

You settle onto the floating lounger that seems to have been custom made for your body. You take a deep breath in and then slowly let it out as you soak up the warmth of the sun and dip your toe in the cool refreshing water. It occurs to you that you are acutely aware of things you haven't noticed in a long time, if ever. You are tuned into your senses. Your breath is flowing slowly and easily. Your muscles are completely relaxed. The sun feels warm upon your face. The water is comfortably cool on your fingers and toes. The air is quiet enough that you can hear the water gently lapping at the edges of your float as well as the nearby birds sweetly chirping their cheerful notes. Every once in a while the subtle fragrance of summer flowers wafts by, and a feeling of contentment envelops you. Your environment has just been transformed from chaos to calm, and as a result, so have you.

If you have ever felt overwhelmed by your environment, you can surely relate to this swimming pool scenario that illustrates the fascinating phenomenon that when your outer world changes from chaos to calm, it has a corresponding effect on your inner world. The two are indeed connected.

Clutter is sneaky. Your space usually doesn't just suddenly become cluttered overnight. Clutter insidiously works its way into your home over time. At first, you barely notice it, then it nudges you every once in a while as a mild irritation when you can't find things that should be at your fingertips: phone, glasses, keys, that document you just had a minute ago...clutter's nudge strengthens into a poke. You notice with more frequency that you are rushed and running late, but you're too busy to slow down and pay attention because there's too much to do and not enough hours in the day to do it. Finally, clutter pushes you to the edge of your proverbial raft. Just when you think you might be in over your head...*phweeeeeet!* You blow the whistle on your clutter. Something must be done.

Often, a stressful situation occurs in our life and builds to a level of overwhelm that becomes the tipping point for inviting change. It wakes us up to a new level of consciousness. Even when we have identified the problem, we don't always know where to begin or how to start solving it. Perhaps we try different tactics that don't work long term, and we eventually revert back to our old ways and finally give up altogether. The mere thought of taking action against our clutter becomes overwhelming, and we find ourselves stuck in an endless cycle that leads to frustration and unhappiness- with ourselves and with others. Yet so often we choose known misery, and we resist unknown joy, because it's easier and safer.

When circumstances beyond our control do not allow us to change our outer world, it can have a negative impact on us and on our lives—if we let it. Yes, we have a choice. Do you choose known misery or unknown joy? Do you choose chaos, clutter, and overwhelm? Or would you rather live a life filled with clarity, peace, and happiness?

With the help of Enneagram wisdom, the dedication to a Mind-Body-Spirit practice, and the commitment to an effective decluttering and organizing method, you can transform your outer world and allow amazing life-changing effects to flow from your inner world. I realize this is easier said than done, but I also know it is doable because I'm speaking from personal experience.

My introduction to the Enneagram was by chance one day when I came across a brief article about it in one of my favorite magazines. I was curious, so I made a note to look it up later. The more I learned about the Enneagram, the more I wanted to know. This is where my life began to shift and I sensed something magical starting to happen. I had never experienced anything like it before, but it was intriguing, exciting, and a little scary all at the same time.

The Enneagram is ancient wisdom that incorporates two of my favorite subjects: psychology and spirituality. It is a powerful tool that can help us discover and understand our True Self. When we are aware of how our personality is influenced by our motivations, we can begin to understand why we respond to the world the way we do and learn to manage our individual strengths and weaknesses.

The Enneagram "helps us become self aware so that we can experience life holistically and honestly" (Rohr)[2]. Because of its depth and dimension, it is difficult to express a basic and concise explanation of what the Enneagram actually is, but Ian Morgan Cron, author of *The Road Back to You*, sums it up simply as "an ancient personality typing system [that] helps people understand

---

[2] Rohr, Richard. "Knowing Ourselves." *Enneagram: Week 1.* Center for Action and Contemplation, 24 April 2016, https://cac.org/knowing-ourselves-2016-04-24/

who they are and what makes them tick" (Cron, 10)[3]. The Enneagram, he explains, "teaches that there are nine different personality styles in the world, one of which we naturally gravitate toward" (Cron, 24).

Richard Rohr, renowned Enneagram master, teacher, and author, explains that the Enneagram is "a dynamic system" and a "powerful tool for self-discovery and spiritual transformation." However, he cautions, "it shouldn't be your only tool. The Enneagram is most helpful when used in conjunction with other practices like study, meditation, spiritual direction, and life in community with others" (CAC Staff).[4] I would add to this list: and an effective method for clearing clutter and organization as well!

In the same season that I was introduced to the Enneagram, and also by chance, I met Michael Rizk, a MindBodySpirit Coach and founder of The Whole Person Project, who, in the course of one casual conversation, dramatically changed the way I perceive myself, my past, my present, and my future. A particularly insightful moment was when he pointed out that by hitting the snooze button every morning, I was starting my day with negativity; essentially saying "no" before I was even awake. I was astounded. I had always thought of myself as a positive and optimistic person. I don't like negativity, and I certainly don't intentionally invite it into my life! Aha! Awareness, Michael enlightened me, is the first step toward making a change. If we're not aware of the problem, how are we supposed to try and solve it? I felt that magical shift again. To quote Ralph Waldo Emerson, "The mind, once stretched by a new idea, never returns to its original dimensions."

I considered this new realization for a few days, and then I began a daily spiritual practice of silence, prayer, mediation, and keeping a gratitude journal- at 5:05 am. No snooze button. It started out as a self-imposed 30-day challenge because I wasn't

---

[3] Cron, Ian Morgan. *The Road Back to You: An Enneagram Journey to Self Discovery.* Inter Varsity Press, 2016.
[4] The Enneagram: An Introduction, Sunday, April 24, 2016, CAC Staff.

really sure what I was doing. To my surprise, I loved it and looked forward to my early morning routine every night when I went to bed. Thank you, Michael Rizk, for teaching me how new seeing leads to new ways of being. Despite all of these positive shifts happening in my life, I was keenly aware of an underlying, constant "unsettled" feeling. I was seeking inner peace and serenity, but my outer world was in a state of flux which was causing my inner and outer worlds to be in conflict. My life was starting to feel a bit overwhelming. I craved a sense of order and the need to simplify my outer world, so I started listening to podcasts, Googling, and reading books on the topics of minimalism, frugality, and home organizing. One day, I left the library laden with an armload of books (the irony not lost on me in my quest for minimizing, simplifying, and decluttering).

I chose to read Marie Kondo's book, *The Life Changing Magic of Tidying Up* first. Its small size, attractive cover, and promising title had caught my attention. Turns out, it was the only book that I had actually needed to bring home that day. I devoured the book in no time, laughing out loud when she not only acknowledged, but debunked every single approach I had ever attempted to become organized. From page one, I felt as if Marie Kondo wrote this book exclusively for me. Ironically at the end she writes, "You … have been led by fate to read [this book], and that means you probably have a strong desire to change your current situation, to reset your life, to improve your lifestyle, to gain happiness, to shine" (Kondo, 203).[5]

The KonMari Method® incorporates gratitude and intention, which especially resonated with me. But what really sold me is the concept that—when followed properly—sorting, decluttering, and organizing is a one-time event. I was so intrigued, a little skeptical, but mostly inspired and hopeful. So I personally put her method to the test. I committed the next 6 months to my KonMari tidying event and practiced Marie's method exactly as she explains

---

[5] Kondo, Marie. *The Life-Changing Magic of Tidying Up*. Ten Speed Press, 14 October 2014.

in the book. Before I began, I followed her advice of spending some time visualizing my ideal lifestyle: countertops and other surfaces free of clutter, a designated space for everything, and a home that contained only things that held a particular purpose or special meaning for me. I resisted the notion of going room by room, a theory that sounds good and plausible, but one in which Marie says makes us prone to failure and rebound, inevitably returning to a cluttered environment.

The KonMari Method® teaches tidying by order of categories: always begin with clothing first, then books, paper, and so on. The purpose of the order is to start with items with the least amount of emotional attachment and continue through to those with the greatest amount, working through sentimental items last. In this way, our ability to make decisions gets easier as we work our way through the categories. I immediately began to see results after my initial efforts with my clothes. My closet felt bigger, the air seemed fresher, and I'm sure it was brighter in there! I can now see at a glance everything I own; it all fits me and is ready to wear. My shoes and bags are on display, like in a boutique. I suddenly understood the feeling to which Marie refers when something "sparks joy." Again I recognized that magical sensation that was becoming more familiar.

The KonMari Method® is about choosing joy. It encourages keeping those things that speak to the heart and letting go with gratitude those that have fulfilled their purpose. Once you have sorted, discarded, and decided what to keep, everything will have a designated space in your home. As with developing any new habit, it is very important to mindfully practice the behavior for lasting success; in this case, intentionally returning items to their place when finished using them. Marie's philosophy is not only proven, but it emphasizes introspection, intention, and happiness. It's about shifting from chaos to calm and will change your life in positive and unexpected ways. You will have free time to spend on what is important to you. Your creativity will flourish. Your goals will come into focus, and your motivation to achieve them will be renewed. Marie writes, "A dramatic reorganization of the home causes correspondingly dramatic changes in lifestyle and perspective" (Kondo, 2-3).

I have come to realize that incorporating several key components into any self-transformational process can lead to profound results. These components include: awareness and intention, visualization and planning, and action and consistency. My personal transformation from chaos to calm has had so many surprising and positive effects in my home and in my life. I have witnessed a shift in my perspective, a reinforcement of my values, and a clarity of my priorities. I have grown to know and understand myself better. My relationship with myself, my belongings, and other people is ever evolving with the awareness to see the world through a wider lens and the ability to express more kindness, acceptance, and compassion for myself and others. I am becoming less anxious, worried, and self conscious, and more relaxed, confident, and connected.

I realize now that the events that seemed to occur by chance during the past few years were what Oprah Winfrey has referred to as "life whispers." Little nudges that try to get our attention because they are important to awakening our purpose. I am more aware, more in tune with my True Self, more awake to the present moment, and all of these whispers contributed to my new way of seeing; my new way of being, that was actually there all along.

I continue to study Enneagram wisdom, participate in Mind-Body-Spirit work, and practice The KonMari Method® of decluttering and organizing, as these three elements together not only enhance, but are instrumental in my personal growth and evolution. The most profound effect of this journey has been taking a leap of faith to become a Certified KonMari Consultant and create a small business to help others discover their potential for transformation through clearing clutter and organizing. I believe anyone has the potential and ability to get and stay organized. With awareness, intention, patience, and commitment, you can transform your outer world and your inner world from chaos to calm. If you live with other people, such as your spouse, partner, family members, or roommates who might not be ready for a tidying event of their own, it's important to remember to lead by example, practice gratitude, and have grace for others as well as for yourself. When people have different values from our own, our awareness and acceptance of that can help bring us peace.

Our homes are not museums or magazines. They provide safety and protection and a happy place to gather with our friends and family; they are meant to be lived in. They tend to get messy at times, and clutter may creep back in. By becoming aware and practicing this method, order can be easily and quickly restored. The same is true in life. Triggers will occur that can cloud our vision and clutter our minds, but with awareness and grace, we are empowered to shift our perspective and choose joy. Chaos is temporary, peace is everlasting.

About Mara Dowler

Mara Dowler is a Professional Home Organizer and Certified KonMari Consultant who has personally experienced surprising, positive, life-changing effects through Enneagram wisdom, Mind Body Spirit work, and the KonMari Method® of decluttering and organizing. Mara created Bluebird Home Organizing, LLC in 2019 in hopes of inspiring others to discover their own life-changing magic. She believes that with the proper tools and guidance, anyone can get and stay organized. Often, the result is so much more than a tidy home; it's a personal transformation from a chaotic lifestyle to a calmer one. Mara happily serves clients along the Connecticut Shoreline, where she lives with her husband and their four sons. Her Enneagram number is 9 with a 1 wing.

www.bluebirdhome.net
mara@bluebirdhome.net

Chapter 15

Making Room to Receive

Elizabeth B. Hill, MSW

This wild thing happens when we let go of the clutter in our homes, minds, and hearts. We begin to receive more abundantly in other aspects of our life. By releasing the clutter, we can release the burden of debt, excess, illness, or weight. We can release things that were not working in our homes, relationships, and businesses. We can receive more of what we need and desire. But we have to make room for it first.

This chapter is specifically about the direct correlation between releasing excess and receiving money. When we release what we don't need or desire, we make room to receive what we *do* need and desire. This chapter is also about how I got the opportunity to question a lot of my money stories along the way of releasing excess and reclaiming my home. I'm using myself as a case study. I'm sharing some stuff that feels super personal. I don't really like airing my dirty laundry, but I feel a desire to share it, because I want you to receive as much as I've received from this process. I want you to be able to get a peek at the spiritual adventure that can be available to us in clearing our homes and embracing our space.

Mindset is Key

Our mindset plays an integral part in our ability to embrace our space and our ability to enjoy our home and possessions. When we are in a scarcity mindset, we could have a million gazillion dollars and be living in fear of losing it all. When we are in a scarcity mindset, even if we are served the fanciest lobster dinner, everything will be wrong with it. We think we always get the worst lobster, the service is poor, and the world has it out to get us. When we are in an abundance mindset, we deeply appreciate our meal (whether it be lobster or a piece of toast) and service (whether it be a first-time waiter who makes a few snafus or a dedicated pro). What we expect to receive, we receive.

When we are in an abundance mindset, we can rest into the knowledge that we are cared for, our needs are met, and we can focus on what we desire. When we are in a scarcity mindset, there's never enough and we live in fear of losing what we have. When we are in an abundance mindset, we care for and cultivate our possessions and money. We honor them. When we are in a scarcity mindset, we abuse our possessions and money, we rack up debt, we hoard possessions or money, we won't share, and we won't receive. There's never enough, but we don't really appreciate what we have.

This scarcity mindset is directly related to decluttering and home organizing. Often, we hold onto objects because we are in fear of losing them. We think there are not enough resources or things or money to go around, and we need to hold onto what we have because at any point we could lose all these things. At some point, we might need this egg-slicer, even though we haven't used an egg-slicer in 15 years, but in some time in the future, we might really, really need it. In an abundance mindset, we can appreciate the egg-slicer and that someone else may be able to enjoy using it right now, and that we have plenty to share, and if we decide we really, *really*, need an egg-slicer in the future, we will be able to have an egg-slicer, but for now we can allow someone else to use it that can enjoy it right away.

The ironic thing is that when we are in fear of losing, when we fear we haven't enough, that is exactly what shows up in our life. We will never have enough. We'll be scraping by, whether we make $30,000, $200,000, or $1 Million in a year.

When we let go, when we release, when we clear, when we

begin to rest into trusting that we will be cared for and taken care of and have our needs met, we begin to receive what is in alignment with our current vibration.

As someone who worked in nonprofits for most of my professional life, money was not something that led my choices. I chose work because it felt like the right thing to do, not because it would be the most lucrative. I made poor money choices because I didn't take care of money and cultivate it. I didn't value it, but I still lived in fear of not having it. No one had enough. The nonprofits I worked for or with didn't have enough. The agencies I worked with didn't have enough. The people I worked with and for didn't have enough. Our clients didn't have enough. No one had any money. I lived just beyond my means, so even as my income rose as my career developed, so did my debt. I was deep in a scarcity mindset. It took a lot of financial and spiritual adventures to bust that mindset up.

Releasing

For those of us who have lived different lives within our lifetime (divorces, break-ups, careers, homes, belief-systems), if we keep holding onto the stuff of our past lives, it continues to vibrate with the energy of the past. These objects are a weight that keep us in that state. Staying in that state and energy can be a choice we make. It is what we know. It is comfortable. There is a comfort in the known, even if it is an unpleasant situation. The unknown, even if it promises a better life, may feel just too scary to step into.

When I moved out of my home in Avon, Connecticut, I faced many of my financial assumptions head-on. I had lived in my home for ten years and it held many stories. It was the place I got to have the little "homestead" I dreamed of. I got to have chickens, my mini-Australian Shepherd/farm dog Lucy, and my children picked peas in the garden. It was where my children started Kindergarten and we took our "first day of school photos" on the porch. It was where I grew my yoga and coaching businesses, where I had a beautiful office with bookshelves, recorded meditations, and where I wrote and published my first book.

I had lived in this home through a marriage and breakup, through living with a roommate with three kids who were fleeing an abusive relationship, and a three-year relationship with a boyfriend who was in active addiction (that despite my years as a social worker I was blind to) and brought the manipulative, destructive behavior of an addict. This house was where I twice had to answer the door to police that were looking for family members. It was a house where I'd lost two pregnancies through miscarriage. Dear Lord, there was such a wild mix of energies in this house. My heart had bloomed and been destroyed there multiple times.

Writing this, I wonder how I didn't leave sooner.

What kept me there? The burden of all the work that it would take to leave. The fear of the unknown. The feeling that I was all alone and no one would help me. The feeling that I didn't deserve the help of others—that I needed to sort this all out on my own.

I finally decided this was not how I wanted to live, that my kids and I deserved better, and that I had to face the work it would take to get out.

I decided to let go of most of my possessions. I started selling things on OfferUp, an app which helps you buy and sell products. I had weird thoughts about this. My brain couldn't shake of the thought that "this is something poor, desperate people do." For some reason, I had it in me that I should be just giving things away. But I began to have fun receiving the money for the things I no longer needed or desired to keep. I was surprised to discover I found I enjoyed meeting the people that were buying the objects. I enjoyed seeing their eyes light up when they were getting just what they were looking for. I discovered that there was not one thing that I sold that I missed.

Things that I didn't sell, I began bringing to Goodwill and handing over. Then came the dumpster. My ex-husband came and went through the house for things he had left when he had moved out – and emptied the entire room above the garage, which held many things we hadn't touched since we moved in. My ex-partner, trying to make amends, came over and helped clear the junk and heavy objects as well.

I brought very little over to my grandma's home: a couple of beds, a couple of bookcases, our clothes, a few end tables, a dresser, two desks, and books. (Oh, my, our arms got strong from carrying the books over.) There was so much I let go of. I estimate I got rid of at least 2/3 of my possessions. I felt free.

Receiving

Once we settled into Grandma's I could sense that our basic needs were met, my client roster scaled through the coaching company I worked for and I landed a coaching client that paid me $4,000 in advance (my previous record was $1800). I began to have money flowing consistently again. If money were water, it felt like the "tap" got turned "on."

I realized at this point that I needed additional help to make the home livable. I'd hit a wall. I'd moved in under a state of crisis, but I didn't want to continue living that way. In order for me to care for my clients, my children, and my grandma, we needed to have a really comfortable, clean, and organized home where we could breathe. I took on my massive clearing and began to receive the support from Embrace Your Space.

I did at least ten trips to Goodwill, plus a run to drop off an unused wheelchair. (I decided we did not need two wheelchairs, when Grandma does not even use a wheelchair. This felt radically against everything I was ever taught by my family. I felt like a revolutionary.) My dad and brother came over to help move out some of the excess. I paid for a company to come and haul out heavy, broken furniture and junk. I felt lighter and lighter.

I brought in Embrace Your Space in September. Once we had cleared the clutter from the main part of the house, the next month (October) my revenue more than doubled (no joke) from $4,653 to $10,597. This was my first ever month of over $10K in revenue. My income was $10K again in December.

I do not think this was a coincidence.

In May of this year, I broke all family lineage messages against having a housecleaner and brought one in. It costs us $150-$200 every other week. Again, as I increased support, my income bumped up again. In May, my business revenue hit $12k and in June it was $12k again.

By releasing the stress and weight of objects and burdens, my mind is free to be openly creative, to focus on my work, enjoy time with family, and be open to receive.

Old me would never have spent money for an organizer or someone to clean my house. But guess what? Old me would never have brought in $12,000 a month either. Playing the old game, I would get the same results. The world needs me to help people honor their stories, the world needs me making books that heal our stories, the world needs me to be there for my family. The world doesn't need me to vacuum. It just doesn't. I'm not good at it and I don't like it and it makes me angry! By bringing people in that enjoy this work—who actually light up while cleaning and organizing—I'm honoring my gifts and their gifts. I'm sharing money with them which helps them meet their needs and build their dreams. And I receive abundance in my own life and business. I receive more time with my kids, more income as I'm able to generate more revenue, and more space to rest and enjoy the life that I've created.

The return on investment (ROI) has been significant in my own personal case study. The money has been significant, but the most significant ROI has been being able to enjoy our home with my family. To be able to enjoy cooking a meal or baking bread in my kitchen, with my favorite cookbooks on the shelf above and with ease because I know where all the ingredients and tools are. To have space to play quadruple solitaire on a clean table with my mom and my kids. To hear my 97-year old Grandma say, "It looks very good in here, doesn't it?" when she walks through the living room. These are the greatest return on investments I could wish for.

My wish is that you will:

1) Realize you have a choice. Keeping your home the way it is is a choice and you also have the ability to choose something else.

2) Don't allow the small payments of a few hundred block you from receiving thousands (or tens of thousands).

3) Open up to receive help and support.

My family and I needed professional help! Cause we aren't organizers! We are creators, we are artists, we are dreamers, we are business-type-entrepreneurial folk. There is no shame in paying people to help you with the things that don't light you up or aren't your skillset.

I still have more to clear—old journals from my youth, toys my kids played with when they were little, letters my great-grandfather received from people I don't know, notebooks of old business ideas, some less-than-ideal furniture we are making do with. I honor the part of me that is not yet willing to part with these gems, and I know that once I do, I will be open to receiving more than I can currently imagine.

Chapter 16

Offering Peace of Mind

Donna Finocchiaro

I have been organizing my entire life and had a wonderful mentor before I even realized how it would impact me later in life. As a child, I would spend summer vacations organizing and re-decorating my bedroom. I remember my mother rearranging furniture in our home on a regular basis, and I am sure it rubbed off on me.

For as long as I could remember, my clothing closet and drawers were always very well-maintained, color-coded, with like items placed together. Socks were always matched, and I would use discarded containers such as tissue boxes to create drawer organizers, a skill I learned from my mother.

Upon entering the workforce, I found myself in structured environments due to my career choice as an accountant where my organizational skills were beneficial to helping me meet deadlines and easily locate important information. I utilized my home-made containers in my desk drawers and color-coded my files. One day, when speaking with a work colleague, he commented how my pens and pencils were lined up like soldiers in my desk drawer. "Doesn't everyone do this?" I thought to myself. It was at this moment when I started to recognize the differences in other people's organizational skills.

Over time, I came to realize I have an innate ability to organize a person's space. My passion about the subject started long before I left the corporate workforce. I would watch episodes of organizing and staging shows on television late at night to clear my mind from the stresses of work. One day on vacation, I had an epiphany. I decided right then and there that I was not going to spend the second half of my working career in an unfulfilling manner. The day I decided to leave my corporate career for self-employment was one of the best decisions of my life.

After making the decision to make a career change, a series of events and opportunities presented themselves that dramatically changed my life. First, I had a wonderful mentor in the industry, who helped me to gain the confidence I needed to start my own business. Then, I was approached by a colleague to co-own an organizing product retail store which created my awareness of senior citizen downsizing. Finally, I was fortunate to open a furniture consignment business in my hometown. It was a short time after that when I realized I had an opportunity, and later a responsibility, to share my skills with others.

I find it easy to trouble-shoot problems on the spot after looking at a space for just a short time. I can open any closet or cabinet and determine the amount of unused space within minutes. Developing the plan to organize the space is another story, however.

It is important to understand what is causing the clutter or disorganization because without this, the fix will likely not be permanent. I often say, "organizers are not like cleaning services" and "we should not need to return to manage the same space if we did our job correctly." In fact, we should be able to transfer our knowledge to others so they can maintain the systems after we are gone. Additionally, no two situations are the same, and believe me, I have seen hundreds over the years. The key is being able to support another person in leading a more streamlined and clutter-free life.

With sixteen years of experience, I have now been self-employed as an Estate Organizer for as long as I was professionally employed. I jumped right into the industry of professional organizing and never looked back. I had found my passion, my driving force in life, and the bonus was that I was helping others to change their lives for the better, too. I am delighted to have helped over one thousand people during this time and I am fulfilling my desire to share my knowledge.

Root Causes/Obstacles

There may be one or many reasons causing an individual to avoid starting the process of organization. A common problem is the embarrassment that comes with having an untidy home. Finances also play a role, as many people feel they cannot afford a service such as this. When my team or I work with a client, we determine where their limitations lie and develop a detailed plan of action to support them. There is no judgment, and a step forward, regardless of how small, is a step in the right direction. Emotional attachment is the greatest issue we see because it can stifle a person from taking action altogether.

Disorganization is often caused by a life-altering event, such as the loss of a loved one, loss of employment, or another tragic situation. When there are several events happening at once, the person may lose interest in organization, cleanliness, or even suffer from low self-worth. In extreme situations, a mental health professional may be needed to assist the team of organizers.

There are certified professional organizers who specialize in chronic disorganization, however, in many situations this is not needed. For us to assist an individual, they must possess the desire to change, be able to pay for the service, and be willing to change their current patterns. If these conditions exist, a person's life can improve dramatically.

At Lotus Transitions, we are skilled at finding creative ways to assist as many people as possible. We expanded our services to cover the state of Connecticut for this reason and have established vendor partnerships in surrounding states to support the work we do. We offer a sense of peace to our clients by working at their pace and addressing their concerns. When finances are the obstacle, we ask the client to provide us with a project budget. From here, we can design a plan to give them the best results for their money. When a person has the drive to change the way they are living, they will often find the financial resources needed so they may start to enjoy a better quality of life and more efficient use of their time.

Benefits of an Organized Life

I believe the effective use of one's time is a key component in leading a holistic life. The benefits of maintaining an organized life are endless and lead to improvements in sleep, lost time trying to find items, better money management, and overall happiness, to name just a few.

Organizational skills have a direct correlation to self-worth and confidence because people often feel there is something wrong with them if they cannot keep a tidy space or home. Others will search for the latest organizing book, hoping to magically transform their lives, while others will head to the latest retail store for excessive amounts of organizing products, thinking these efforts will fix their problem, only to be met with much disappointment. There is one key component missing from this approach, which is the customization needed to effectively create permanent change. This is why individuals who organize professionally need to constantly assess the situation and pivot when needed to achieve the desired result.

Speaking from personal experience, I believe I would not have had the financial success in business without my extreme organizing abilities. I say extreme because I have what I refer to as obsessive compulsive "tendencies." It troubles me to leave a project unfinished and I often work at something until I achieve the best result possible. The standards I set for myself are usually greater than those around me which allows me to achieve better than expected results.

My physical health is positively impacted also because I sleep well at night knowing I have assisted my clients to the best of my abilities. Restful sleep and efficient processes equate to having more personal time, which directly leads to a better quality of life.

Everyone can achieve better organization in their life, despite not being born with the organizing "gene." Practicing daily organization and starting small are the keys to success. An additional bonus to a successful outcome is having someone who will help you stay on task, such as a friend, mentor, or coach who can identify the signs when obstacles get in the way or you are feeling less than motivated. Sometimes, an encouraging word is all it takes.

I have created a take-action journal entitled "30 Days to Better Organization" which includes my top ten organizing tips, areas to capture a small task per day, and to record the feeling surrounding the experience, as well as providing encouragement throughout the book.

The premise of the journal is that it takes a person 21 days, or repetitions, to create a change in habit. I have extended this to 30 days to ensure success. When a person regularly keeps at a given task for this amount of time, they often find themselves falling into autopilot, where the task becomes easier by the moment, and hence, more enjoyable. The purpose of journaling throughout the process is to capture the feeling, whether positive or negative, to identify the reasons for failure or success. Getting to the root cause of disorganization is critical to moving past the problem.

My favorite tip is to start small and by that, I mean a single drawer or shelf or as little as a corner of a room. Often, I hear people say, "This weekend I am going to organize my basement... or my garage." These areas are much too big to take on without a structured plan. A successful outcome also requires a healthy mental attitude about the project. Starting with a positive vision about the result, including how it will make you feel, contributes to the overall success of the project. I recommend giving this a try because I am confident you will be pleased with your results.

About Donna Finocchiaro

Donna Finocchiaro is an entrepreneur and businesswoman who is general manager for her home-grown professional organizing company, Lotus Transitions, LLC. She utilizes innate skill sets and acquired knowledge daily in supporting others state-wide. In 2004, Donna left the fast-paced world of finance to pursue her passion of bringing home organizing solutions to the public. She began her career as the managing director for another company, and after 18 months and 100% growth, an opportunity presented itself to collaborate with a colleague to open an organizing product retail store. Through her unique collaborations and entrepreneurial thinking, Donna continually finds new solutions for her clients. The vast array of services provided by the company, and the caring manner in which the team operates, are what makes Lotus Transitions unique and highly sought after.

On a personal note, Donna prides herself on community involvement, supporting local small business owners and entrepreneurs like herself. Her major contributions include her work as a member of two chambers of commerce and a local rotary club where she heads committees and serves on boards. Over the years, Donna has helped more than one thousand people through hands-on help, mentoring, or professional speaking. The company has a specialty niche in supporting the senior citizen marketplace with downsizing, and also handles home organization, staging and selling unwanted items. Donna was honored to be an active member of two Extreme Makeover: Home Edition CT builds and spearheads a team that supports hundreds of inner-city school-aged children each year.

www.LotusTransitions.us

Chapter 17

An Invitation

Elizabeth B. Hill, MSW

Facing the daunting task of home organizing can feel overwhelming. I spent endless hours stressing over it, making plans over it, and bought many books about it before I was able to take it on in earnest.

Try this meditation: Sit in a comfortable place where you can relax. Take three deep, slow breaths in and out. Imagine standing at your front door. Imagine opening the door and looking in and having it look exactly the way you want it to be. What would greet you? Who would greet you? What are the scents you smell upon your arrival? What path do your feet meet as you enter? What art is on the walls? Where are your favorite places to sit? To do work? To talk with friends? To share a meal? To cozy up and relax? Breathe with these images and feel as though you are already there. Now, grab a notebook. Take notes. Write down what it felt like to be in this space.

Now, reach out to one of the pros in this book for support. They are outside of your circle. They can hold your vision without letting family dynamics or other obstacles get in the way. What might feel like an unscalable mountain to you, will feel like a little speed bump to them. They have helped many people navigate challenges before and can do the same for you. Share your beautiful vision of what you'd like your home to be, even if you have no idea how you could make it happen. They can help you.

If one of the author's stories resonated with you, please reach out to them. Those of us who have gone through this tend to form an easy kinship. Where others may blame or shame or judge, we get it. You can drop the shame, the stress, and the weight you are carrying. Some people are deeply passionate about helping people get their homes in order. It brings them immense joy. Why not let them? Why hold it and carry it yourself?

I invite you to embrace your space. And to let others embrace you, too, a bit. Life doesn't have to be so hard. And you don't need to go it alone. We got you.

Love & Courage,

Elizabeth

About Green Heart Living

Green Heart Living's mission is to make the world a more loving and peaceful place, one person at a time. Green Heart Living Press publishes inspirational books and stories of transformation, making the world a more loving and peaceful place, one book at a time.

Whether you have an idea for an inspirational book and want support through the writing process—or your book is already written and you are looking for a publishing path—Green Heart Living can help you get your book out into the world.

You can meet Green Heart authors on the Green Heart Living YouTube channel and the Green Heart Living Podcast.

www.greenheartliving.com

Green Heart Living Press Publications

Be the Beacon

Grow Smarter: Collaboration Secrets to Transform Your Income and Impact

Amla Speaks 365

Redefining Masculinity:
Visions for a New Way of Being

Your Daily Dose of PositiviDee

Transformation 2020

Transformation 2020 Companion Journal

The Great Pause: Blessings & Wisdom
from COVID-19
The Great Pause Journal

Love Notes: Daily Wisdom for the Soul

Green Your Heart, Green Your World:
Avoid Burnout, Save the World and
Love Your Life

Made in United States
North Haven, CT
11 November 2021